THIS BOOK
BELONGS TO

. . . .

For Great Aunty Betty and Harold.
Both inspiring in their own special way.

———— ⋰⊰❈⊱⋱ ————

Creative Directors **Hannah Read-Baldrey & Christine Leech**
Art Director & Designer **Christine Leech**
Stylist & Illustrator **Hannah Read-Baldrey**
Photographer **Tiffany Mumford**

For Quadrille Publishing
Editorial Director **Jane O'Shea**
Creative Director **Helen Lewis**
Project Editor **Lisa Pendreigh**
Production Director **Vincent Smith**
Production Controller **James Finan**

First published in 2011 by
Quadrille Publishing Ltd
Alhambra House
27–31 Charing Cross Road
London WC2H 0LS
www.quadrille.co.uk

British Library Cataloguing-in-Publication Data
A catalogue record for this book is available from the British Library.

ISBN: 978 184400 972 5

Printed in China

Everything Alice

Quadrille
PUBLISHING

contents

Welcome

to the wonderful world of Alice, where all is not what it seems

This book began as a little idea, a little idea hatched within an ordinary conversation over a cup of tea. We were having a chat – stood at the bottom of a staircase in a location house, which was dressed as Christmas day even though it was July – and simultaneously we both exclaimed how we would love to make a craft book with the theme of Alice in Wonderland. Years later you are now holding our first book in your hands… and we couldn't be prouder!

To create *Everything Alice* we spent the summer months preparing all the projects: we sketched out ideas on napkins in pubs and cafés; we got dirty collecting old bits of furniture from skips to revamp into stunning Fabric-Covered Furniture (see pages 66–67); we rummaged through London's finest charity shops to buy tea sets for our Vintage Cake Stand (see pages 92–93); we selected beautiful fabrics for all of our fantastic sewn projects, including The Dandy White Rabbit (see pages 14–17); and we delved into craft shops for everything in between. Our partner-in-crime, Tiffany Mumford, took the beautiful photographs in this book. We all worked hard to get each image just right: it was great fun setting up the larger scenes, such as the Shadow Puppet Theatre (see pages 58–61), which was a truly magical experience.

Most of the photographs were shot at Hannah's parents' stunning home, for which we have to give special thanks. After visiting Christ Church, Oxford and the gardens Alice herself played in, we couldn't have found a better alternative! Whilst photographing we were lucky with the weather, except the day of the croquet game. That day the August heavens opened causing sodden playing cards, damp fabric hedgehogs and the paint to run on the flamingos that took Christine's father and us hours to make, never a good look…

Once the photographs were taken, Hannah returned to her kitchen table to create the intricate papercut illustrations dotted throughout this book while Christine began the mammoth task of designing the book so that every page is perfectly Alice.

Everything Alice is the creative must-have for any Alice lover and an enticement for those who are yet to fall down the rabbit hole. We do hope you love this book as much as we do!

~ ON THE ~
TRAIL OF ALICE

One November morning we wrapped up warm and caught a train to Oxford for a trip to Christ Church, part of the town's renowned University, and to take a look around the home of Charles Dodgson, aka Lewis Carroll.

At 11am we were announced by the tinkle of the bell on the heavy wooden door of Alice's Shop, an old building on St Aldate's. This shop would have been known to Carroll and, as it is situated opposite the University, he is sure to have visited. We battled our way through the extraordinary collection of Alice-related trinkets, from plastic rulers to handmade chessboards, and both bought something; it was hard to resist.

It was here local historian Mark Davies kindly took us on a tour that brought Carroll's Victorian Oxford back to life. In 1851 Carroll read Maths and Classics at the University before staying on to become a reverend. He met and befriended the Dean's three daughters, Lorna, Edith and Alice Lidell, and they often spent time punting along Oxford's waterways. During these outings Carroll created wondrous stories; one such tale was Alice Underground, which the real Alice persuaded him to write down. This became the story we know and love today!

Do you know many of the characters from the tales were based on real people and places? Familiar references are still scattered around the University: reflections of the Cheshire Cat can be found in the chapel where there are a selection of gruesome gargoyles carved into the stone arches, one of which appears to be a smiling cat. Within the wooden panelled Great Hall are two central fireplaces, both appointed with golden firedogs with comical elongated necks; one can't help but assume these were the inspiration for Alice's neck to grow.

Even Alice's Shop is mentioned in *Through the Looking Glass* when the story tells of a room suddenly filling with water. On first glance this seems pure fantasy, however in the December of 1852 the flooding of the low-lying ground near the waterways was so bad that this parade of shops could only be accessed by boat via the first-floor windows.

Carroll was inspired by the people he met everyday. It is thought the Queen of Hearts was based on Alice's governess, Mary Prickett: "The very essence of all Governesses." The White Rabbit may have been Alice's father, Henry; at that time Oxford worked on its own time that was five minutes later than GMT; that's why the White Rabbit was always late. A recent theory suggests the Mad Hatter was fashioned on Mr Randell, a local tailor and mayor. His house sits oddly on arches over the river with chimney pots that look like a pair of March Hare's ears! Even the famous croquet game was a reference to when the Royal Family came to visit.

Our trip to Oxford gave us a fantastic insight into the world of Alice; if you get the chance, go!

'The time has come,' the Walrus said, 'To talk of many things: Of shoes and ships and sealing-wax Of cabbages and kings And why the sea is boiling hot And whether pigs have wings.'

CRAFT KIT

A good craft kit is like a magpie's nest; full of little scraps of fabric, paper and sparkly things that may be useful one day.

Scissors: *Never use scissors for cutting both paper and fabric; they will stay sharper longer if they only do one job. Small embroidery scissors are useful for snipping stray threads, while pinking shears create decorative edges.*

Glues: *PVA glue is useful for many projects as an adhesive and a sealant. A glue-gun is great for fixing things fast, while specific glues for fabric, paper and ceramic are also useful. Glue dots come in all shapes and sizes and are a clean and easy way to fix things.*

Tapes: *Sellotape, invisible, masking and gaffa tape.*

Craft knife or scalpel

Wire cutters

Staple gun

Stapler

Paper fasteners

Wallpaper paste

Mosaic grout

Sewing machine

Sewing needles: *A good selection of needles with various size holes and thicknesses, including ones for embroidery. A big blunt needle with a large eye is very useful for threading ribbon or elastic through hems.*

Pins

Threads: *Various cotton and silk threads for sewing and embroidery.*

Buttons & beads: *Of all shapes and all sizes.*

Scraps of ribbon & fabric: *For decoration.*

Silver garden wire

Tailor's chalk or fading pen

Tape measure

Steel ruler

Assorted paint brushes

COOKERY KIT

Quality cookery utensils will not only last you years but will help you achieve perfect results.

Kitchen scales & measuring spoons

Wooden spoons

Measuring jug

Sieve

Whisks: *Electric, balloon or food processor.*

Rubber spatula: *Perfect for cleaning bowls.*

Rolling pin

Mixing bowls: *Big ones for cakes and small ones for icing.*

Baking tray: *Best with edges, for extra grip when removing from a hot oven.*

Cupcake or muffin tin

Foil, clingfilm & baking paper

Cooling rack

Jam thermometer

Cocktail sticks

Cupcake cases

Piping bags: *Disposable ones are best to reduce mess.*

Piping ends: *A 1cm nozzle for macaroons and a selection of smaller star and writing ends for decoration.*

Knives: *Bread knife and other sharp knives.*

Selection of cutlery

TIME FOR TEA JEWELLERY

The miniature furniture and accessories designed for dolls' houses
make great charms for this most curious jewellery.

For the bracelet
medium-weight gold chain
wire cutters
medium and large gold jump
rings
1 toggle clasp
dolls' house tea set or other
miniature items and charms
an assortment of glass
and diamanté beads
headpins
seed beads
2 pairs of round-nose pliers

The beauty of this jewellery is that each piece is unique: it's a great way to use up all those odd beads and little charms that are bought on a whim or are left over from other projects. Tiny buttons, sequins and bells look lovely interspersed with beads and a miniature tea set – pretty much anything with a hole in it can be hung on a chain!

Bracelet

Using the wire cutters, cut a 19cm length of gold chain. Next, using jump rings, attach one part of the toggle clasp to each end of the gold chain.

To plan your design, lay the chain out in a line and place your beads and charms beneath it until you are happy with the order. We suggest placing a large charm, such as a teapot, in the centre of the bracelet and then adding approximately two beads between each medium charm, such as a teacup.

For beads with a hole through their middle, thread a seed bead onto a headpin followed by the bead and another seed or smaller bead. Using round-nose pliers, make a wrapped loop (see overleaf). For the tea set, buttons and any beads with a hole through the top, attach them to a jump ring.

Using jump rings and following your design, attach the beads and charms to every other link of the chain. The more beads and charms you add, the more jangly the bracelet but also the heavier!

continued

~ Time For Tea Bracelet ~

— Time For Tea Earrings —

Earrings

For the earrings
lightweight gold chain
wire cutters
1 pair earring wires
headpins
2 small jump rings
various glass and crystal beads
2 pairs of round-nose pliers
dolls' house tea set

⁓ Using the wire cutters, cut two 2.5cm lengths of gold chain. Attach an earring wire to the last link of each chain.

⁓ For each earring you will need about five small beads plus little crystals or diamantés to provide some extra sparkle. Attach the beads to the chain by hooking the loop of the headpin through a link of the chain before completing a wrapped loop (see below). Attach the beads to alternate sides of the chain links.

⁓ Finally, attach a teacup or milk jug to the bottom link of the chain using a small jump ring.

HOW TO MAKE WRAPPED LOOPS

1 Thread the beads onto the headpin. Using round-nosed pliers, form a loop leaving a small stem of headpin above the beads.

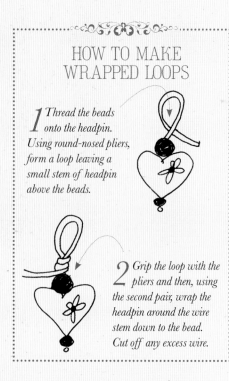

2 Grip the loop with the pliers and then, using the second pair, wrap the headpin around the wire stem down to the bead. Cut off any excess wire.

— Time For Tea Necklace —

Necklace

For the necklace
5mm gold jump rings
headpins
80cm lightweight gold chain
a selection of beads
seed beads
2 pairs of round-nose pliers
wire cutters
dolls' house tea set

⁓ Join the two end links of the chain with a jump ring. Attach your teapot to this ring. Hang a variety of beads and charms on either side of the teapot. You may prefer the teapot and just one other bead on your necklace, or you could fill the entire chain.

"Alas for poor Alice! when she got to the door, she found she had forgotten the little golden key; and when she went back to the table for it, she found she could not possibly reach it: she could see it quite plainly through the glass, and she tried her best to climb up one of the legs of the table, but it was too slippery; and when she had tired herself out with trying, the poor little thing sat down and cried."

DRINK ME

THE DANDY WHITE RABBIT

Lovingly create your own handsome White Rabbit toy. He looks super-dashing in
his suit, accessorised with a bow tie and pocket watch; perfect for the rabbit about town!

For the White Rabbit
1m white velvet fabric
20cm floral print medium-weight cotton fabric, for ears
matching sewing thread
1 large bag of soft toy stuffing
2 black buttons, for eyes
pink embroidery thread,
for whiskers

For his suit
50cm blue print cotton fabric
30cm pink print cotton fabric,
for jacket lining
matching sewing thread
2 floral buttons, for jacket
75cm length of 2.5cm-wide
pink grosgrain ribbon, for bow
tie (optional)

For his pocket watch
20cm white felt
blue embroidery thread
15cm narrow blue ribbon

Note: The seam allowance is
1cm throughout.

Warning: Do not use small
parts, such as buttons, if you
are making this toy for a
small child as they can be a
choking hazard.

To make the White Rabbit

✒ Using the templates on page 134, cut two of each of the following from the white velvet: head, ears and body. Cut four of each of the following from the white velvet: arms and legs. From the floral print cotton cut a further two ears for the inners. Transfer any markings from the templates to the fabric.

✒ To join the arms and legs, place together two of the velvet pieces with right sides facing. Pin and tack. Stitch around the sides with a 1cm seam allowance, leaving the top edge open. If necessary, clip the curved seams. Turn right side out (if it helps, use the handle of a wooden spoon). Press flat. Fill firmly with toy stuffing, packing evenly from the hands and feet upwards.

~ stuff the arms & legs ~

~ attach the ears ~

✒ To make the ears, place together one white velvet piece and one floral print cotton piece with right sides facing. Stitch around the sides, leaving the bottom edge open. Turn right side out. Press flat. Fold each of the sewn ears in half along their length so only the white velvet is showing. Pin together on the fold in the same direction.

✒ To attach the ears to the head, lay out one of the head pieces flat with the right side facing upwards. Place the folded ears on the point marked "A", aligning the raw edges. Place the second head piece on top with the right side facing downwards. Pin and tack. Stitch around the sides, leaving the neck edge open. Turn right side out. Press flat. Fill the head firmly with toy stuffing.

continued ☞

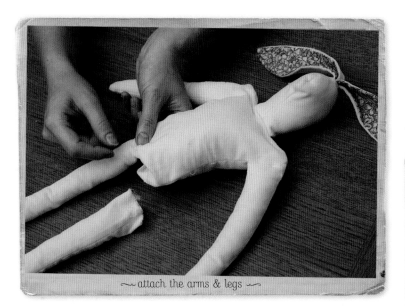

~ attach the arms & legs ~

To make his suit

✏ Using the templates on page 135, from the blue print cotton cut two trousers (on the fold), two jacket fronts and one jacket back (also on the fold). From the pink print cotton cut two jacket linings. Remember to flip the jacket front and lining templates to cut one left side and one right side.

~ make the suit jacket ~

✏ To attach the arms to the body, lay out one of the body pieces flat with the right side facing upwards. Place one stuffed arm on the point marked "B" and the other on the point marked "C", aligning the raw edges. Place the second body piece on top with the right side facing downwards. Pin and tack. Stitch along the sides only. Turn right side out.

✏ To attach the head, press under a 1cm hem along the body's top edge. With the central front seam lined up with point "D", place the head into the pressed seam on the body. Pin and tack. Topstitch along the shoulder line. Fill the body with toy stuffing.

✏ To attach the legs, press under a 1cm hem along the body's lower edge. With the central front seams facing forward, place a leg at either side of the body's bottom edge. Topstitch all along the bottom line.

✏ Add two black buttons for eyes. Add whiskers to his nose by knotting and fraying a length of pink embroidery thread.

✏ Place together the two trouser pieces with right sides facing. Pin and tack. Stitch along the outer and inner sides, leaving the top and bottom leg edges open. Turn right side out. Press flat. Press under a 1cm hem around the waistband and topstitch down. Stitch a 1cm double hem on each trouser leg, ensuring the raw edges are not visible.

✏ Place together the jacket linings and fronts with right sides facing. Pin and tack. Stitch along the shoulder, front and lower edges only. Turn right side out. Press flat.

✏ Press under and stitch a 1cm hem along the neck and lower edges of the jacket back. Place together the lined front jackets and the jacket back with right sides facing. Pin, tack and stitch. Turn right side out. Press back the lapels to reveal the lining. Dress your Dandy White Rabbit in his suit and stitch on two jacket buttons.

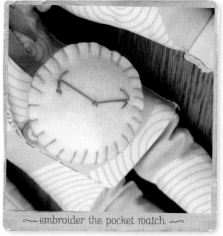

To make his pocket watch

Using the template on page 134, cut two pocket watch pieces from the white felt. With blue embroidery thread, hand sew 5mm-wide blanket stitches just over half way around the watch-face (see page 24). Lightly fill the watch with a small amount of toy stuffing. Continue stitching around the watch-face until it is completely closed. With pink embroidery thread, add the fast and slow hands.

Attach a length of blue ribbon to the back of the watch. Stitch the top of this ribbon to his suit jacket, just under the lapel.

And there you are, your Dandy White Rabbit is complete. Give him a kiss!

"Oh my ears and whiskers, how late it's getting!"

HEART LETTER HOLDER

Cherish your precious postcards and letters with love.

2 sheets white A2 mount board
1m x 50cm of 3cm-thick
wadding
stapler and staples
60cm x 60cm toile de jouy or
other medium-weight cotton
hot glue-gun
5m of 5mm-wide ribbon
12 brass paper fasteners
12 fabric-covered buttons,
1.5cm in diameter
40cm length of garden wire

Draw out a heart template about 40cm wide by 40cm tall, and use it to cut two heart shapes from the mount board.

Fold the wadding in half so it is double thickness. Using one of the heart-shaped boards as a template, trace the heart outline on to the wadding. Draw a second heart outline 3cm all around outside the first. Cut out the larger heart. Lay out the cut wadding flat and place one heart-shaped board on top. Fold the edges of the wadding over the heart-shaped board and staple in place, pulling it taut. Trim any excess wadding.

Lay out the print cotton fabric flat, with the wrong side facing upwards. Trace the heart outline on to the fabric, then draw a second outline 10cm all around outside the first. Cut out the larger heart. Place the wadding-covered board on top of the fabric heart, with the wadding side down. Using a hot glue-gun, adhere the fabric to the reverse of the board, pulling it taut. Start with the straightest sides, then clip and notch the fabric so it lays neatly around the curves.

Lay lengths of ribbon across the heart board, equally spaced in 10cm intervals. Place four in left-slanting diagonals and four in right-slanting diagonals to make a lattice pattern. Leave an extra 10cm of ribbon at each end. Where the ribbons cross, using a scalpel or bradawl pierce a small hole

~ cover the board ~

~ fix the ribbons ~

through the board. Push a brass paper fastener through each hole and secure at the back. Take the excess ribbon ends over to the reverse of the board and glue in place, pulling taut. Using a hot glue-gun, cover each fastener head with a fabric-covered button.

To make a hanging hook, pierce two holes in the second heart-shaped board in the upper centre, about 15cm apart and level horizontally. Feed a length of wire through these holes and wrap the ends around themselves to secure.

Line up both of the heart-shaped boards, with reverse sides facing. Using a hot glue-gun, adhere the boards together, tucking any raw fabric edges neatly inside.

DRESS-ME ALICE
& WHITE RABBIT

Have splendid fun dressing up Alice and the White Rabbit in outfits fit for the Royal Court, a tea party or even a boating trip down the river.

You will need
thin card
PVA glue
scissors

Colour photocopy these pages. Glue the copy onto a sheet of thin card. Carefully cut around both characters, their clothes and accessories.

Fold the card backwards along each dotted line on Alice's and the White Rabbit's stands and the tabs on their clothing.

Stand up and dress.

LAVENDER DORMICE

*These sleepy dormice are scented with dried lavender, which is a natural moth repellent.
Hang them by their tails in your wardrobe or nestle them in your knicker drawer.*

You will need

small amount of fabric, such
as velveteen, for mouse's
body, tail and outer ears
small amount of contrasting
print fabric, for mouse's
bottom and inner ears
matching sewing thread
tailor's chalk
toy stuffing
dried lavender (approx
1 tablespoon per mouse)
ribbon, for decoration
small button, for decoration
dark embroidery thread,
for eyes

~ attach the bottom ~

Note: The seam allowance
is 5mm throughout.

Warning: Do not use small
parts, such as buttons, if you
are making this toy for a
small child as they can be a
choking hazard.

☛ Trace and cut out the templates on page 128. Fold a 20cm x 22cm piece of the mouse's body fabric in half widthways with right sides facing. Place the body template on the fabric and draw around it with tailor's chalk. Pin both sides of the fabric together. Stitch from points "A" to "B", via the nose. Trim the excess fabric close to the line of stitching and up to the chalk mark on the open edge.

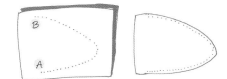

☛ Using the bottom template, cut one bottom piece from the contrasting print fabric. Align point "B" of the body with point "C" of the bottom and points "D" on both the body and bottom. Pin and tack. Stitch down both sides, leaving the lower edge open.

☛ Turn the body right side out and fill with a mixture of toy stuffing and lavender. As the body is stuffed, the fabric around the hole turns in on itself creating a neat edge. When plump, hand sew to close the opening.

Tail 1

Tail 2

☛ There are two ways of making the mouse's tail. If you are using a fabric with a bit of stretch, like fleece or velveteen, cut a 30cm x 4cm rectangle. Fold the fabric in half lengthways with right sides facing. Starting at one corner, stitch diagonally across to the opposite corner. Trim the excess fabric close to the line of stitching. Turn right side out. This can be fiddly with such a small tube, so use a pencil to poke the fabric out. If you are using a stiffer fabric, like cotton or linen, follow the same method but stitch the tail fabric together with the wrong sides facing. Trim the excess fabric with pinking shears. Hand sew the tail to the mouse's bottom using a small button for decoration.

☛ Place a 10cm x 7cm piece of each of the velveteen and contrasting print fabric together with right sides facing. Using the ear template, draw two ears on the wrong side of the print fabric. Pin and tack. Stitch around the curved sides, leaving the lower edge open. Trim the excess fabric closely around the stitch line. Turn right side out. Turn inside the raw edges to neaten and press. Pinch each ear together at the base to create a mini dart. Secure with a couple of stitches. Hand sew ears to body. Finally embroider onto the mouse's head sleepy eyes in dark embroidery thread using a few backstitches (see page 24). Decorate your mouse with ribbons.

"'The Dormouse is asleep again,' said the Hatter, and he poured a little hot tea upon its nose.

'I wasn't asleep,' he said in a hoarse, feeble voice: 'I heard every word you fellows were saying.'"

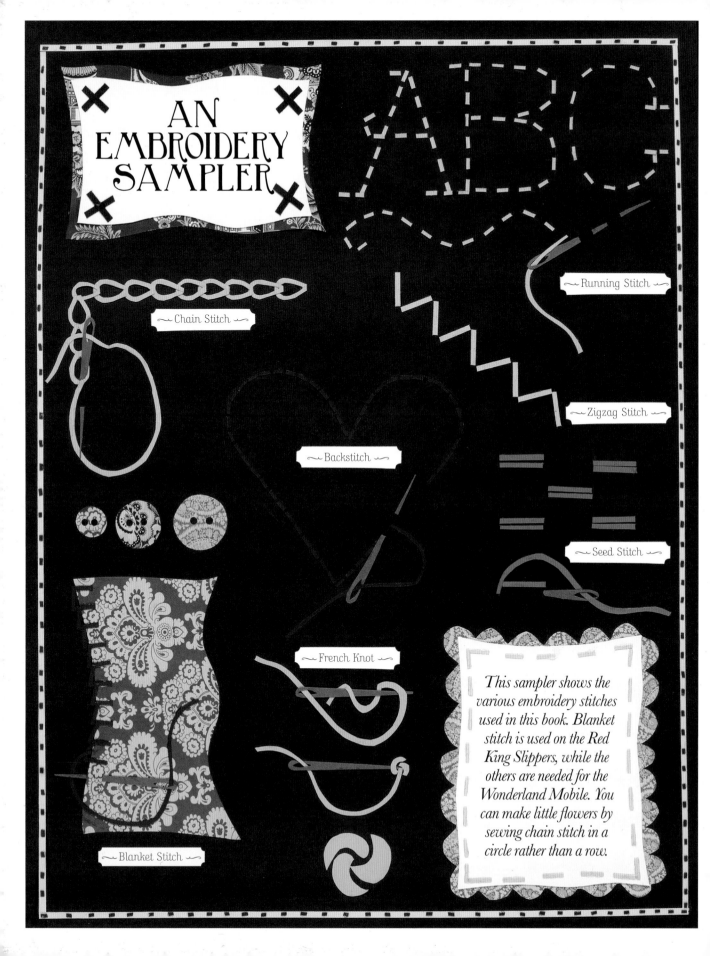

AN EMBROIDERY SAMPLER

ABC

~ Chain Stitch ~

~ Running Stitch ~

~ Backstitch ~

~ Zigzag Stitch ~

~ Seed Stitch ~

~ French Knot ~

~ Blanket Stitch ~

This sampler shows the various embroidery stitches used in this book. Blanket stitch is used on the Red King Slippers, while the others are needed for the Wonderland Mobile. You can make little flowers by sewing chain stitch in a circle rather than a row.

INVITATION CUSHION

This cushion is a real invitation to have a sit down and a bit of a rest. It can be personalised with a name or a full address. By adjusting the size and type of fabric used, you can turn the case into a purse, make-up bag or even an elegant clutch.

For the cushion
1m x 50cm oatmeal linen
1m x 50cm print cotton, for lining
matching sewing thread
40cm x 30cm cushion pad

For the decoration
pink embroidery thread
10cm x 6cm white felt
10cm x 8cm pink velvet
40cm length of small pompom trim
scrap of narrow pink satin ribbon
small decorative button
black embroidery thread
multicoloured sequins
30cm length of gold ricrac
20cm length of 4cm-wide striped grosgrain ribbon
large gold button

Note: The seam allowance is 1cm throughout.

~ make the basic envelopes ~

Using the template on page 136, cut two envelope shapes; one from the linen outer fabric and one from the cotton lining fabric.

Fold the cotton lining envelope in half where marked with right sides facing. Pin and tack. Starting at the lower edge, stitch up each side, finishing 5mm before the top edge. Repeat with linen outer envelope. Turn the linen outer envelope right side out.

Slip the outer envelope inside the lining envelope, with right sides facing. Pin and tack around the lower curved envelope opening (1) and the envelope flap (2).

~ 1 ~

~ 2 ~

Stitch around the opening and flap, leaving 10cm unstitched along one straight edge – this is the turning hole.

With sharp scissors, clip the corners and notch the curved seams so that the envelope lays neatly when pressed.

Turn the envelope right sides out through the turning hole, then ease the lining down into the outer envelope.

Press all the seams, easing the fabric at each curve to give a nice rounded shape.

~ turn the cover right sides out ~

continued ☞

To decorate

☞ Embroider onto the front panel your chosen name and, if preferred, address in pink embroidery thread using backstitches.

☞ Using the template on page 136, cut out a Queen's head silhouette from the white felt. Adhere the felt Queen's head to the small rectangle of pink velvet with fabric glue.

☞ Place the pompom trim around the edges of the velvet, covering all the raw edges. Pin and tack. Stitch around all sides.

☞ Decorate the Queen's head by adding a ribbon bow for her sash, a small button for her earring and embroidering a small French knot (see page 24) in black embroidery thread for her eye.

☞ Using a fine brush, paint the shape of a crown in fabric glue on the Queen's head. Sprinkle sequins onto the glue crown, then press so they stay in place. Shake gently so any loose sequins fall off. Alternatively, if the cushion is going to be frequently laundered, use a length of sequinned ribbon or hand sew individual sequins in place for the crown.

☞ Place the stamp on the front panel of the cushion in the top right-hand corner. Pin and tack. Stitch around all sides. Cut three lengths of gold ricrac. Stitch or glue the ricrac over the stamp for the postage mark.

☞ Machine stitch or hand sew onto the lower back panel a diagonal line from both outside corners to the centre of the opening.

☞ In the centre of the flap, machine stitch or hand sew a buttonhole. Fold the length of striped ribbon in half at a slight angle. Snip diagonally across both ends. Place the gold button with the folded ribbon beneath to align with the buttonhole. Sew in place to make the Royal seal. Finally, fill with a cushion pad and deliver to a worthy recipient.

"The Fish-Footman began saying, in a solemn tone,
'For the Duchess. An invitation from the Queen to play croquet.'
The Frog-Footman repeated, in the same solemn tone,
'From the Queen. An invitation for the Duchess to play croquet.'"

WANT TO BECOME A QUEEN?

Can you believe as many as six impossible things before breakfast? If so you might have what it takes to become a queen. With instruction from REAL QUEENS (Red & White) you can learn the correct etiquette, deportment and manners. Packed full of hints, tips and useful lessons, this postal course proves ANYONE can become a Queen!

A LESSON IN DEPORTMENT
by the Red Queen

1 "Look up, speak nicely, and don't twiddle your fingers all the time."

2 "Curtsey while you're thinking what to say, it saves time."

3 "Open your mouth a little wider when you speak, and always say 'your Majesty.'"

4 "Always speak the truth – think before you speak – and write it down afterwards."

5 "Speak in French when you can't think of the English for a thing – turn out your toes as you walk – AND REMEMBER WHO YOU ARE!"

THE WHITE QUEEN'S PATENTED EXERCISE TO PREVENT CRYING

"Consider what a great girl you are. Consider what a long way you've come to-day. Consider what o'clock it is. Consider anything, only don't cry!"

"*That's the way it's done,*' says the Queen *'nobody can do two things at once, you know.'*"

COULD *YOU* BE A QUEEN?
take our test to find out

Addition
Q. What is one and one and one and one and one and one and one and one and one and one?

Subtraction
Q. Take nine from eight.

Q. Take a bone from a dog: what remains?

Division
Q. Divide a loaf by a knife – what's the answer to that?

Languages
Q. What is the French for fiddle-de-dee?

ANSWERS **Addition** 10, unless you lose count. **Subtraction** Trick question, it's not possible. The dog's temper would remain. The dog would lose its temper. Then if the dog went away, its temper would remain! **Division** Bread-and-butter. **Languages** Fiddle-de-dee is not English, find out what language "fiddle-de-dee" is, then find the French for it!

A satisfied customer says:

" *WELL, this is grand! I never expected I should be a Queen so soon. I was afraid the crown might come off, but I shall be able to manage it quite well in time.* **"**

Alice Liddell, 7 and a half exactly

SEND NO MONEY NOW
PAYMENT ONLY ON CORONATION

QUEEN ALICE BAG

This bag is the perfect size for carrying a sandwich and your favourite
"Alice In Wonderland" tales down to the river for a little adventure...

For the bag
1m x 50cm oatmeal linen
1m x 50cm print cotton
matching sewing thread
1m length of 4cm-wide striped
grosgrain ribbon, for the strap
strong sewing thread

Note: The seam allowance
is 1cm throughout.

For the decoration
20cm x 15cm white felt
22cm x 18cm pink velvet
84cm length of medium
pompom trim
medium decorative button
black embroidery thread
multicoloured sequins
length of 1cm-wide gold ricrac
20cm length of 4cm-wide
striped grosgrain ribbon
scraps of ribbons

☞ Using the template on page 137, follow the instructions on page 26 for the Invitation Cushion to make the basic envelope.

☞ Place one end of the shoulder strap ribbon on the inside flap of the bag, just above the opening. Pin and hand sew the end in place using a strong thread. To reinforce the stitching, sew a rectangle, then sew diagonal lines between the corners. Take care not to sew through to the linen outer envelope. Repeat with the other end.

To decorate
☞ Using the template on page 136, cut out a Queen's head silhouette from the white felt. Place the head in the centre of the rectangle of pink velvet. Pin and either machine stitch or hand sew with blanket stitches around the Queen's head.

☞ Follow the instructions on page 28 for adding the pompom trim, button earring, embroidered eye and sequinned crown. Use a wider brush to apply the fabric glue for the crown for more sequins. Stitch the stamp on the front panel of the bag, add the postage mark to the stamp and embroider the extra lines on the envelope back in the same way.

☞ Follow the instructions on page 28 to add the buttonhole, button and ribbon.

☞ If the bag gets dirty, sponge clean with a little warm water.

~ Queen Alice Bag ~

WHITE RABBIT & CHESHIRE CAT MASKS

These masks are great fun for parties and masquerade balls.

You will need
PVA glue
white mosaic grout
tile clippers
hot glue-gun

For the White Rabbit
1 sheet of white A2 mount board
10mm square mosaic tiles: 230 white, 110 cream, 90 pink (approximate quantities)
35cm length of 5mm dowelling rod, for the handle
white acrylic paint

For the Cheshire Cat
1 sheet of black A3 mount board
10mm square mosaic tiles: 120 black, 50 grey (approximate quantities)
35cm length of 5mm dowelling rod, for the handle
black acrylic paint

❧ Using the templates on page 137, cut two of your selected mask shape from the mount board. Paint your dowelling rod the corresponding mask colour – white for the rabbit and black for the cat – and allow to dry.

❧ Cover your work surface with a protective sheet as mosaic work can be messy! Apply a small blob of PVA glue to the back of each mosaic tile and adhere to the first mask shape, leaving a 2mm space between each tile. Get creative and make up your own pattern. Trim away any overhanging tiles with the clippers. Allow to dry thoroughly for at least two hours.

❧ As an alternative to ready-made 10mm mosaic tiles, make your own small tiles from old pots and crockery in your required colours. Wrap the crockery in a few sheets of newspaper, then place into a thick plastic bag. Make sure you put the bag on a durable surfaces before smashing the crockery into small pieces with a hammer. Remove the pieces carefully from the wrapping as they will be sharp.

❧ Mix the white mosaic grout to the manufacturer's instructions in a jam jar or plastic container. Keep a bowl of water and a sponge nearby. Using your hands, spread the grout over the mosaic, working it into the spaces between each tile. Try to keep the surface of the grout as smooth as possible. Leave the mask on a flat surface and allow the grout to dry fully. It's best to leave it overnight.

❧ Once dry, wipe down the mosaic with a damp cloth to remove any excess grout. Allow to dry for a further few hours, then give it a final polish with a soft cloth.

❧ With a hot glue-gun, stick the second mask shape onto the back of the tiled one, sandwiching the dowelling rod in between (on whichever side of the mask you prefer).

HOW TO RUN
A CAUCUS RACE
by the Dodo

1 A Caucus race is the best thing for getting oneself dry after a soaking, or to warm oneself on a winter's day. It can be run indoors or outside, by however many people are present.

2 Mark out a sort of circle around trees or furniture, the exact shape does not really matter. Each participant can start the race wherever they choose around the course.

3 The pleasure of a Caucus race is that there is no "One, two, three and away". Everyone can begin running when they like and let off when they like (good for smaller creatures). Some critics say it is not easy to know when the race is over.

4 After half an hour or so someone must call out "the race is over" and then there will be prizes.

5 The joy of this race is that everyone is a winner. Suitable prizes are comfits and thimbles.

SUGAR & SPICE COMFITS

The Victorian comfit was a nut, seed or piece of spice covered in hard sugar, rather like the sugared almonds of today. Often they were used as a breath freshner. These comfits are less laborious to make than the Victorian version, but just as tasty.

It's the caraway, fennel and coriander seeds that give these comfits their unique flavour, so it's up to you what other nuts and dried fruit you use. Apricots, pistachios and ginger each have a lovely jewel-like colour that make the comfits look delightful.

250g mixed nuts
50g sunflower seeds
1 tablespoon coriander seeds
1 tablespoon fennel seeds
1 tablespoon caraway seeds
100g dried fruit
caster sugar

✆ Place a thin layer of the nuts and seeds on a baking tray and toast under a medium grill, shaking continually, until they are just browning on all sides. Remove from the heat and allow to cool.

✆ Add the dried fruit to the nuts and seeds, chopping any large fruits into smaller pieces.

✆ Now for a bit of magic. When we first heard of this method, we really didn't believe it would work – it's real kitchen alchemy. Sprinkle a layer of caster sugar into a frying pan, just deep enough so that it covers the base of the pan. Place over a low heat, watching carefully for the magical moment the sugar simply disappears and turns into a syrup. Remove from the heat straightaway and immediately stir in the fruit and nuts, making sure they are all evenly covered by the sugar syrup. Take care as the syrup will be extremely hot.

✆ Cover a baking tray with greaseproof paper and spread the caramelised comfits over the tray to cool. The sugar syrup will have stuck the fruit and nuts together in clumps; if any are particularly large, gently break them up into daintier morsels.

✆ These comfits are a great snack to take on walks and tasty sprinkled over ice cream. Store in an airtight container for up to a week (but they don't last that long in our house).

"The next thing was to eat the comfits: this caused some noise and confusion, as the large birds complained that they could not taste theirs, and the small ones choked and had to be patted on the back."

DRINK ME CORDIALS

These cordials are simple to make, but to an extent they rely on personal tastebuds!
When mixing the final drink, you may want to add extra sugar and dilute to taste.

"Tied round the neck of the bottle was a paper label, with the words 'DRINK ME' beautifully printed on it in large letters. It was all very well to say 'Drink me,' but the wise little Alice was not going to do that in a hurry.

'No, I'll look first,' she said, 'and see whether it's marked "poison" or not'… She had never forgotten that, if you drink much from a bottle marked 'poison,' it is almost certain to disagree with you, sooner or later. However, this bottle was not marked 'poison,' so Alice ventured to taste it, and, finding it very nice (it had, in fact, a sort of mixed flavour of cherry-tart, custard, pine-apple, roast turkey, toffy, and hot buttered toast), she very soon finished it off."

Lavender Lemonade

The addition of lavender to this lemonade brings a modern twist to a perennial favourite.

250g sugar
300ml lemon juice
14 stems fresh lavender

☞ Add the sugar to 500ml of water and boil until disolved. Add the lavender and remove from the heat. Cover the pan and leave to infuse the sugar syrup.
☞ When cool, add 500ml water and the lemon juice. Strain to remove the lavender.
☞ Serve with crushed ice and garnished with lavender flowers.

Strawberry & Raspberry Refresher

For an adult drink, adding a shot of vodka to this juice makes a refreshing summer cocktail.

300g frozen raspberries	300g sugar
200g fresh strawberries	50ml lemon juice

☞ Place the fruit and sugar into a pan. Cook over a medium heat for 20–25 minutes, stirring occasionally, until the sugar is dissolved and the fruit is pulpy.
☞ Mash the fruit, then strain the mixture. Do not push the fruit through the strainer as that will give a cloudy juice. Be patient!
☞ Discard the pulp. Add the lemon juice to the fruit syrup. Add 1 litre boiling water. Leave to cool, then refrigerate.
☞ Serve with crushed ice and garnished with mint leaves.

Pear & Ginger Cordial

This cordial is deliciously warming on a winter's day when served hot.

300g sugar	1 teaspoon cream of tartar
1 large ginger root	150ml lime juice
1 piece lime rind	2 pears

☞ Add the sugar, chopped ginger, lime rind and cream of tartar to 400ml water and boil for 5 minutes. Add the lime juice.
☞ Return to the boil, then add the peeled, chopped pears. Simmer until softened. Mash the pears to a pulp then strain.
☞ Store in a sterilised bottle and keep refrigerated. Serve diluted to taste.

Elderflower & Rhubarb Cordial

Pick fresh elderflowers in early summer. For the rest of the year, use shop-bought cordial.

500g sugar	1 sliced lemon
20 elderflower heads	3 sticks rhubarb

☞ Add the sugar to 1 litre of water and boil until dissolved. Remove from the heat.
☞ Place the elderflowers (shaken to remove any bugs) and sliced lemon into a container. When cool, pour over the sugar syrup.
☞ Cover with a cloth and leave to infuse the sugar syrup for at least two days or longer for a stronger flavour. Stir regularly.
☞ Place the chopped rhubarb into a pan and strain over the elderflower cordial. Bring to the boil, then simmer until the rhubarb is soft. Leave to cool then strain.
☞ Store in a sterilised bottle and keep refrigerated. Serve diluted to taste.

"*Tied round the neck of the bottle was a paper label, with the words*

DRINK ME

beautifully printed on it in large letters."

HUMPTY DUMPTY DOORSTOP

Keep your door open in style with this sleepy Humpty, a perfect gift for an Un-birthday present. *

For Humpty Dumpty
1m x 1m medium-weight or heavyweight white cotton
1m x 1m medium-weight or heavyweight cotton ticking
matching sewing thread
toy stuffing
1 large plastic sandwich bag
approx 2.5kg split peas or rice, for filling
10cm x 10cm red fabric, for cheeks
red and black embroidery thread
3 buttons (optional)
1.5m length of 5cm-wide velvet ribbon (optional)

For his hat
1 sheet of medium-weight A4 black card
50cm x 50cm black cotton
20cm length of 1cm-wide red ribbon, for bow

Note: The seam allowance is 1cm throughout.

Warning: Do not use small parts, such as buttons, if you are making this toy for a small child as they can be a choking hazard.

~ prepare the pyjamas ~

Using the templates on page 132, cut one tab on the fold and then four of each of the following from the white cotton: body, arm and leg. Cut four of each of the following from the cotton ticking: pyjama body, arm and leg. Snip each body piece at points "T", "B", "A" and "L".

Turn up a 1cm double hem on all the pyjama pieces at the waist, wrists and ankles. Pin and stitch. Lay out the white pieces flat with the right sides facing upwards. Place the hemmed pyjama pieces on top with the right sides facing upwards. Pin and stitch. To join the arms and legs, place together two of the pieces with right sides facing. Pin and stitch around the sides with a 1cm seam allowance,

~ 2 ~

leaving the top edge open. Turn right side out (if it helps, use the handle of a wooden spoon). Press flat. Fill firmly with toy stuffing, packing evenly from the hands and feet upwards.

To attach the arms and legs to the body, lay out one of the body pieces flat with the right side facing upwards. Place one stuffed arm and leg on each of the points marked "A" and "L", aligning the raw edges and making sure the hands and toes point upwards. Pin and stitch. Join the other body pieces together. Pin one body piece to a second along one side only with right sides facing; line up points "T" and "B" and the waistband of the pyjamas. Stitch. Attach the third body piece in the same way.

~ 1 ~

~ stitch together the body ~

continued ☞

"'Must a name mean something?' Alice asked doubtfully
'Of course it must,' Humpty Dumpty said with a short laugh:
'my name means the shape I am —
and a good handsome shape it is, too.
With a name like yours, you might be any shape, almost.'"

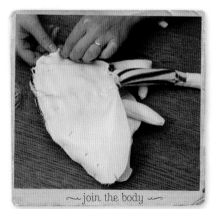

~ join the body ~

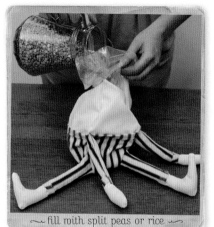

~ fill with split peas or rice ~

☞ To join all the body pieces, pin the one with arms and legs attached to the sewn three with right sides facing and positioning the limbs inside the body. Join as before, lining up points "T" and "B", but this time stitch along both sides.

☞ Turn the body right side out, poking the arms and legs through the turning hole at the top. Place the plastic bag over your fist and push your hand through the hole inside the body. This forms the lining so the split pea or rice filling will not get damp. Using a jug, carefully pour the filling into the plastic bag. Once the body is nicely full, tie the bag into a firm knot.

☞ To make the tab, turn under a 1cm hem on both long sides and press. Fold in half lengthways, aligning hemmed edges, and topstitch. Fold the tab in half to make a loop then place in the opening at the top of the body, tucking the edges of the opening under to neaten. Pin and stitch across the tab to close the opening.

☞ Embroider the face with whatever expression you prefer – our Humpty has sleepy eyes embroidered in black thread. We added small red discs of fabric edged in blanket stitch for his cheeks with a chain stitch mouth. Add any other finishing touches of your choice – we gave our Humpty some pyjama buttons, velvet ribbon trims and a simple rosette.

To make his hat

☞ Using the templates on page 132, cut from the black card one of each of the following: hat top, side and brim. Lay out the black fabric flat with right side facing downwards on top of a sheet of newspaper. Apply PVA glue to one side of the card pieces then adhere to the fabric, leaving a 1.5cm margin around each shape. Allow to dry. Cut out the shapes plus the 1.5cm margin. Clip the excess fabric, then pull taut over to the reverse of the card and glue in place. For the hat's side, trim the excess fabric from one short side. Roll the hat into a tube, overlapping the remaining excess fabric over the other short side and glue in place. Fold the long sides over and glue taut. Allow to dry (use a paperclip to hold the tube together until dry). Join this tube to the hat's top and brim with a glue-gun. Tie a length of red satin ribbon into a bow around the brim. Glue-gun the finished hat to Humpty's head.

"*Humpty Dumpty sat on a wall:*
Humpty Dumpty had a great fall.
All the King's horses and all the King's men
Couldn't put Humpty Dumpty in his place again.

———⊰❈⊱———

'That last line is much too long for the poetry,'
Alice added, almost out loud, forgetting that
Humpty Dumpty would hear her."

CHESHIRE CAT HAND WARMER

Keep snuggled with a cute microwaveable lavender-scented hand warmer.

You will need
25cm x 25cm medium-weight print cotton
two pieces 25cm x 25cm cotton jersey
tailor's chalk or soft pencil
matching sewing thread
10cm x 10cm 1cm-thick cotton wadding
approx 500g rice, for filling
4 dried lavender heads (optional)
2 non-metallic buttons, for eyes
non-metallic embroidery thread

Warning: As you will be heating this in
the microwave, do not use any metallic
buttons or threads.

Lay out one square of cotton jersey flat, place the second on top with the right side facing upwards then place the print cotton on top of them both with the right side facing downwards. Pin together and press flat. Using the template on page 131, trace the outline of the cat's head onto the reverse of the print cotton. Stitch all the way round the outline, leaving a 3cm opening at the lower edge for the turning hole. Trim any excess fabric after it has been sewn (otherwise the jersey has a tendency to move about), leaving a seam allowance of 1cm.

~ stitch the head ~

Turn the head right side out through the turning hole, ensuring the two jersey layers are to the back and the print cotton to the front. Press flat.

~ quilt the ears ~

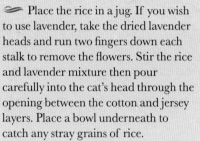

~ fill with rice ~

~ embroider the face ~

✎ Using the template on page 131, cut two ear shapes from the cotton wadding. Insert them into the cat's head through the opening and manipulate each wadding piece so they sit snugly in each ear. Machine stitch or hand sew along the quilting lines as marked to create a padded effect.

✎ Place the rice in a jug. If you wish to use lavender, take the dried lavender heads and run two fingers down each stalk to remove the flowers. Stir the rice and lavender mixture then pour carefully into the cat's head through the opening between the cotton and jersey layers. Place a bowl underneath to catch any stray grains of rice.

✎ Hand sew the opening closed then, following the guide on page 131, add the cat's nose, mouth and whiskers in black embroidery thread using small backstitches. Add two mis-matched, non-metallic buttons for eyes.

✎ You can now heat up your cute cat. Place it in microwave at 800 watts or a medium-high heat for 2 to 3 minutes.

CUPCAKE EMBROIDERY BOX

The charm of this box is that it works at many different sizes. A small cupcake makes a perfect gift box for something special whilst larger ones are great embroidery or jewellery cases – the soft icing top is perfect for storing either pins or brooches.

For the case

1 sheet 3mm-thick A3
buff or white card
masking tape
35cm x 15cm print cotton
scrap of felt, for base
35cm x 20cm fabric, for lining
thin double-sided tape
PVA glue, watered down
8cm length of 4cm-wide ribbon

For the lid

42cm x 13cm white stretch
cotton jersey or fleece
white embroidery thread
polyester toy stuffing
ribbons and beads,
for decoration
7cm length of thin ribbon and
small button, for fastening

For the cherry

20cm x 10cm red fabric
12cm x 6cm green fabric
10cm x 5cm brown felt
pipecleaner
embroidery thread
polyester toy stuffing

To make the case

↶ Using the templates on page 127, cut one of each of the base and sides from 3mm-thick buff or white card. If you are using pale fabrics to cover the case, a darker shade of card may show through.

↶ Roll the sides piece into a conical shape, overlapping the short edges by approximately 2.5cm. Fix the join securely with masking tape. If necessary, reinforce this join with another narrow piece of card.

↶ Slip the base piece into the sides so that it sits snugly at the bottom. Fix the base piece to the sides using masking tape. Keep this neat so there are no bumps to show through.

↶ reinforce the side join ↶

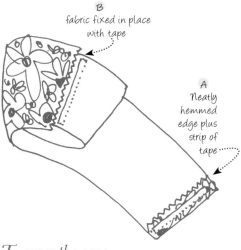

B
fabric fixed in place
with tape

A
Neatly
hemmed
edge plus
strip of
tape

To cover the case

↶ Using the template on page 127, cut out one sides piece from the print cotton adding a 1cm seam allowance all the way round.

↶ Turn under a 1cm hem at one short edge of the sides fabric (see A). Fix in place with double-sided tape. Starting at one side of the join, fix the unhemmed short edge of the sides fabric to the card case with more tape (see B). Wrap the length of the sides fabric around the case, aligning top and lower edges and overlapping the raw edge with the hemmed edge. Fix in place with more tape.

↶ Clip the 1cm seam allowance all the way round both the top and lower edges, spacing each cut approximately 1cm apart.

continued

To make the lid

☞ Using the template on page 127, cut an inner and outer lid from the white card.

☞ Turn under a 2cm hem along one long side of the white jersey fabric. Press and stitch. To join the tube, fold the fabric in half widthways with right sides facing and stitch along the short edges, stopping 5mm before hemmed edge. Pass a length of embroidery thread through the gap in the hem, leaving an extra 10cm of thread at each end.

☞ Slip the larger card disc into the fabric tube and position it 3cm in from the unhemmed lower edge. The stretch of the fabric holds the card in place. Take this 3cm over to the base of the card disc and glue in place.

☞ Place the lid on a flat surface. Fill the fabric tube with a large handful of toy stuffing, adjusting the amount until it looks right. To gather the lid, draw up the lengths of embroidery thread as tightly as possible. Do not worry about the small hole left in the "icing" as this will be covered by the cherry. Decorate the icing with ribbons and beads.

☞ Cut the disc of lining fabric using the template. Snip 5mm cuts around the circumference. Spread a thin layer of glue onto the smaller card disc and cover with the lining fabric, taking the excess fabric to the reverse side.

~ cover the case ~

~ glue the lid base ~

~ gather the lid ~

~ line the case ~

☞ Run a strip of tape around the inside rim of the case, very close to the top. Fold the fabric over to the inside and fix on the tape – the cuts in the fabric allow it to overlap giving a smooth finish. Repeat at the base.

☞ To prevent the box slipping on smooth surfaces, cut a disc of felt the same size as the base using pinking shears. Glue in place.

To line the case

☞ Using the template on page 127, cut one disc from the lining fabric. Snip 5mm cuts around the circumference. Spread a thin layer of glue onto the inside base of the case and a little way up the sides. Place the fabric disc inside the case and press. Allow to dry.

☞ For the hinge, cut one 8cm length of 4cm-wide ribbon. Glue the first 3cm of ribbon to the inside of the case at the join.

☞ Using the template on page 127, cut one sides piece from the lining fabric using pinking shears. Spread a thin layer of glue onto the inside of the case. Place the fabric inside the case and press. Allow to dry.

"Soon Alice's eye fell on a little glass box that was lying under the table: she opened it, and found in it a very small cake, on which the words 'EAT ME' *were beautifully marked in currants."*

~ attach the cherry ~

To make the cherry

➥ Trace and cut out the templates on page 127. Fold the red fabric in half widthways with right sides facing. Place the cherry template on the fabric and draw around it with tailor's chalk. Pin both sides of the fabric together. Stitch along the curved sides, leaving the top open for a turning hole. Trim the excess fabric close to the line of stitching and up to the chalk mark on the open edge. Turn right sides out and press. Turn under the open edges and press. Repeat with the green fabric and leaf template.

➥ To make the stalk, fold the brown felt in half. Place the straight edge of the template along the fold. Stitch along two sides. Trim the excess fabric close to the line of stitching. Insert the pipecleaner and twist into shape.

➥ Hand sew a line of running stitches around the opening of the cherry. Fill with toy stuffing and then pull the stitches up tight. Before the hole closes completely, stitch the leaf and stalk to the inside of the cherry. Tie the gathered threads tight. Pull the leaf down and hold in place with a few stitches. Sew the cherry to the lid covering the hole in the icing.

~ join the lid ~

To join the lid and case

➥ Align the seam of the lid with the join of the case. Place the lined lid disc in the centre of the lid, covering any untidy edges and sandwiching the ribbon hinge between the lid and the disc. Glue in place. If you want to add a button and ribbon fastening to the front of the case, sandwich a 7cm loop of narrow ribbon between the lid and disc, then hand sew a button to the case to match.

WONDERLAND MOBILE

You will need
2 small tree branches, one slightly larger than the other
a selection of felt squares in various colours (we've used mainly white, red, pink, beige, purple, yellow, blue and brown, but it's useful to have scraps of several other colours for the smaller details)
fabric glue
a selection of embroidery silks in contrasting colours
a selection of small buttons and tiny seed beads
polyester toy stuffing
gold embroidery thread, for hanging cords, cut into 50cm lengths

Note: When gluing the felt pieces in place, use a thin layer so you can still push the needle through the glued felt.

The bold shapes and intricate embroidery of this mobile will delight and entertain a young baby for hours. Each motif is so special that you could easily make just one or two of your favourites either to stuff with wadding and use as pin cushions or fill with lavender to make into scented sachets.

Unless otherwise stated, each motif is identical on both sides, so whatever you do on one side be sure to do on the other. When attaching a hanging cord, sew it in the centre of the motif so it hangs straight from the twig.

TO CONSTRUCT THE MOBILE
Making a mobile that is balanced and hangs evenly involves a bit of trial and error. Often it is easiest to construct the mobile in the place where it will hang. Fix a small hook in the ceiling. Tie the larger of the two tree branches to this hook with a length of strong thread – start by tying the branch in its middle, but this may need adjusting to get the branch to hang level. Tie the smaller branch from the larger branch. Attach a hanging cord to the centre of each motif. Hang the White Rabbit from the centre of the smaller branch, then add the other motifs. You'll need to adjust each motif to keep them balanced. To attach the Cheshire Cat to the larger branch, either use strong adhesive and glue him in place or attach a cord and wrap the thread around the branch to secure.

White Rabbit
Using the templates on page 125, cut two each of "A", "C", and "E" from white felt. Cut two "B" from blue felt. Cut one "D" from yellow felt. Glue the inner ears "B" in place. Following the stitch guide on page 126, embroider the inner ears, flowers and eyes on both "C" pieces, but embroider the pocket watch on just one. Embroider the flowers on both "E" pieces. Sandwich piece "D" between the two "E" pieces. Secure with a small stitch.

To join the rabbit, place the larger tail piece only in between the two body pieces. Starting above the tail, hand sew straight stitches around the outer edge. At the ears, attach one of the outer ears "A". Continue stitching to just before the tail, leaving a small opening. Fill with toy stuffing. Hand sew the opening closed. Sew the second ear piece "A" in place.

"All in the golden afternoon
Full leisurely we glide;
For both our oars, with little skill,
By little arms are plied,
While little hands make vain pretence
Our wanderings to guide"

Mushroom

Using the templates on page 124, cut two "A" from red felt. Cut two "B" from beige felt. Cut two "C" from white felt. Glue the flesh "B" and stalk "C" in place. Following the stitch guide on page 126, embroider the decoration and add the buttons.

To join the mushroom, starting at the base, hand sew straight stitches around the outer edge, leaving a small opening. Fill with toy stuffing. Hand sew the opening closed.

Cupcake

Using the templates on page 124, cut two "E" from white felt. Cut two "D" from pink felt. Cut two "C" from green felt. Cut two "B" from red felt. Cut one "A" from purple felt. Glue the icing "D" in place on the case "E". Following the stitch guide on page 126, embroider the decoration. Embroider the decoration on both "B" pieces. Sandwich piece "A" between the two "B" pieces. Secure with a button on each side.

To join the cupcake, place the larger cherry piece only in between the two icing pieces. Starting at the base, hand sew straight stitches around the outer edge, leaving a small

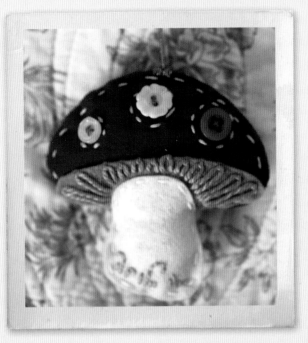

opening. Fill with toy stuffing. Hand sew the opening closed. Sew the leaf "C" in place.

Crown

Using the templates on page 124, cut two "C" from orange felt; two "B" and four "D" from red felt; two "E" from white felt; and one "A" from purple felt. Glue the inner crown pieces "D" and brim "E" in place. Following the stitch guide on page 126, embroider the decoration. Sandwich heart "A" between the two "B" pieces. Secure with a small stitch.

To join the crown, place the larger heart piece only in between the two crown pieces. Starting at the base, hand sew straight stitches around the outer edge, leaving a small opening. Fill with toy stuffing. Hand sew the opening closed.

Heart

Using the templates on page 125, cut two "A" from purple felt. Cut two "B" from pink felt using pinking shears. Glue the smaller hearts "A" in place. Following the stitch guide on page 126, embroider the decoration.

To join the hearts, starting on a straight side, hand sew straight stitches around the outer edge, leaving a small opening. Fill with toy stuffing. Hand sew the opening closed.

Cheshire Cat

Using the templates on page 125, cut two each of "A", "B", "C" and "F" from brown felt; two of "E" and one of "H" from pink; two of "D" from green; and two of "G" from orange. Glue "E", then "G" to each ear "F". Glue the head and tail and to each "A", and the flower and leaves to one "A". Following the guide on page 126, embroider the body and tail on both sides, but embroider the face and ears on just the one.

To join the cat, hand sew straight stitches around the outer edge, leaving a small opening and catching in the ears between two head pieces. Fill with toy stuffing. Hand sew the opening closed.

"Thus grew the tale of Wonderland; Thus slowly, one by one
It's quaint events were hammered out, And now the tale is done,
And home we steer, a merry crew, Beneath the setting sun."

HOW TO DECORATE AN EGG

1.

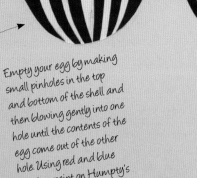

Empty your egg by making small pinholes in the top and bottom of the shell and then blowing gently into one hole until the contents of the egg come out of the other hole. Using red and blue acrylics, paint on Humpty's stripey pyjamas.

2.

Using a fine brush carefully paint on Humpty's face.

3.

Enlarge the accessories below to 150% on a colour photocopier and glue onto thin card. Cut out the shapes and stick to your egg Humpty using small glue dots.

GIANT ROSE LIGHTS

Win first prize this year for the best roses with this spectacular display of easy-to-make lights. If you cannot get hold of strings of large bulbs, you can easily make smaller roses for fairy lights.

You will need

1 string of 10 outdoor LED globe lights
5 sheets of A2 red card
5 sheets of A2 white card

Warning: To avoid any fire risk, use only outdoor LED lights with these light shades. As they are made from card, these rose lights are suitable for outdoor use only in good weather but can be used indoors.

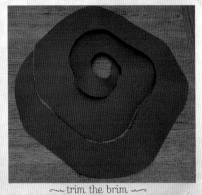

~ trim the brim ~

~ start the rose ~

☞ Cut a 42cm diameter disc from each sheet of card. Find the centre point. With paper scissors, cut a rough spiral shape starting at the outer edge and working into the middle. Keep the lines of the spiral between 10cm and 14cm apart, but it is fine to have a slight wave to the edges.

☞ Cut a small hole in the very centre of the spiral. Feed your light bulb through this central hole in the card spiral. With the first section of the card spiral, form a cone around the bulb and staple to secure, avoiding all wires.

~ staple in place ~

~ repeat for each shade ~

☞ Continue spiralling the card around the bulb. Staple the shade at further points to secure, twisting and tightening as you go.

☞ Repeat for each rose, alternating between red and white card. For greater impact, make more than one string of lights.

SHADOW PUPPETS

You will need
2 sheets of A4 black card
1 sheet of A2 white card
10 wooden kebab skewers
4 brass paper fasteners
a torch
an old pillowcase

To make the puppets
Trace the templates on these pages onto the black card. Cut out each shape carefully. To make the Alice puppet, join the hands and arms to the shoulders using brass paper fasteners at the marked points. Glue the wooden skewers to Alice's arms and legs so they face side out. Attach wooden skewers to all the other shapes to use as rods for manipulating the puppets.

To make the theatre
Photocopy the curtains on these pages, glue to the white card and cut out. Cut a rectangle to the size of the theatre from the pillowcase. Glue to the card. Cut two 10cm-tall card triangles. Attach to the theatre's reverse side for support. Place the torch behind the theatre, turn the lights out and it's showtime!

TEACUP CANDLES

Curiouser and curiouser as Alice once said... These candles make a lovely and unusual gift or table centre for your Mad Hatter's Tea Party. Fine bone china teacups work best as the thinness of the china lets the light shine through as the candle burns.

You will need
old teacups
candle wax (approx 250g of wax will fill approximately four average-sized teacups)
tacky wax (for attaching the wicks to the base of the teacups)
wire-filled wicks with metal clip bases
candle thermometer
old saucepan
old food cans
wax fragrance and colours (optional)

Fill your teacup with hot water to warm it, so it won't crack when you pour in the hot wax. Choose a length of a wick that is at least 2cm greater than the height of your teacup. Add a blob of tacky wax to the metal base of the wick and fix it to the base of the teacup.

Make a simple water bath in which to melt the wax. Place an old food can inside an old medium-sized saucepan; if you squeeze one side of the can slightly to create a spout the wax will pour more easily. If your wax has come as a block, chop it into small chunks. Place the wax chips in the can. Fill the saucepan with 5cm of water. Place the

saucepan over a medium heat and bring the water to the boil, making sure the water doesn't enter the can. If you wish to add fragrance or colour to the wax, do it now following the manufacturer's instructions. Heat the wax, checking the thermometer and making sure it never boils. Once the wax has reached the required temperature, remove from the heat.

Pour the wax carefully into the teacup. Use an oven glove to hold the can and pour slowly, holding the cup at a slight angle to prevent any air bubbles from forming. Make sure the wick remains as upright as possible.

As the wax cools, it may sink a little around the wick. If this happens, fill the dip with a little more wax as the candle sets for a level finish. Leave the candle to harden overnight then light, enjoy and daydream.

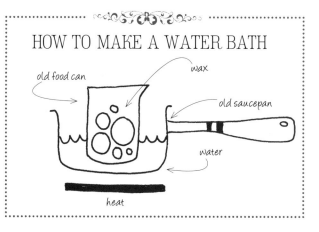

HOW TO MAKE A WATER BATH

old food can

wax

old saucepan

water

heat

FABRIC-COVERED TEAPOTS

Create a colourful home for your blooms! These eccentric teapot planters brighten up any windowsill.

You will need
teapot – any size or colour
PVA glue
50cm x 50cm print cotton
waterproof matt varnish
compost
bedding plants

~ cut the fabric into strips ~

~ start with the spout ~

☞ Clean your teapot and remove the lid. Cut some of your fabric into a few small strips around 5cm wide and 10cm long. In a plastic cup mix your PVA glue; one part glue to one part water.

☞ Beginning with the spout and handle, paint the glue directly onto the teapot then onto the fabric strips. Wrap your fabric carefully around the teapot, trimming any excess pieces as you go.

~ cover the teapot's body ~

~ varnish the teapot and display ~

☞ Now work on the body, it is best to cut longer strips around 1cm wide. Once fully covered allow to dry. A good tip is to place your teapot on a kitchen cooling rack so the air can get to the bottom.

☞ Once dry, paint the fabric-covered teapot with a layer of waterproof matt varnish. Fill the teapot with potting compost and plant.

FABRIC-COVERED FURNITURE

There is nothing more fabulous than transforming an old boring piece of furniture into a masterpiece by covering it in a bright fabric. Believe it or not all of this stunning furniture was taken from skips or donated by people who were throwing it away. Also it's a great opportunity to use up old bedspreads, duvet covers and other colourful scraps of material. We brought it all back to life with this very simple – slightly messy – but ultimately very effective method. One of our favourite sayings when doing this project was "everything looks better with a pompom trim!"

You will need

an old piece of furniture
brightly coloured patterned fabric
wallpaper paste
pompom trimmings and tassels
waterproof varnish

❧ Clean your item of furniture ensuring there is no dust, dirt, loose nails or sharp edges.

❧ Mix up wallpaper paste in an old bucket and cut fabric into long strips. Dip the fabric strips into the paste and squeeze away excess. Wrap the strips around the legs and fiddly bits of furniture. For flat areas cut the material roughly to shape, dip in paste and stick down. Use a painter's brush to smooth the material down and remove excess paste.

❧ Allow to dry. If you are planning on leaving any of the furniture outside, then apply a couple of coats of waterproof varnish.

❧ When dry, go to town with your pompom trimmings and tassels.

> "*Alice thought she had never seen such a curious croquet-ground in her life; it was all ridges and furrows; the balls were live hedgehogs, the mallets live flamingoes, and the soldiers had to double themselves up and to stand on their hands and feet, to make the arches.*"

HOW TO PLAY CROQUET
by the Red Queen

1 In the absence of flamingos and hedgehogs a traditional croquet set can be used. To begin, appoint one person the Queen and one person in charge of hoops.

2 The Queen must decree "Off With Their Heads" at least once a minute as and when she sees fit. The chosen person then leaves the game immedietly. The hooper can change the hoop positions when ever they please.

3 This is a very fast-paced version of croquet. Everyone begins at once and can use any ball available. The aim of the game is to get through all the hoops before being beheaded.

TOPIARY CUPCAKES

These unusual cupcakes are a great show piece for any celebration.

You will need

12 shop-bought chocolate cupcakes
200g fondant icing sugar
400g royal icing sugar
12 round candy lollipops
edible green glitter
green food colouring
red food colouring
1 large orange cut in half

Makes 12 cupcakes

Lay out your 12 cupcakes on a tray. To make the grass, mix up the fondant icing sugar by adding water, its best to follow manufacturer's instructions. Add a few drops of the green food colouring. Lightly dust your work surface with the icing sugar and roll out. With a cookie cutter cut 12 rounds, approximately 4cm in diameter. Brush the backs with water and stick to the top of the cupcakes.

For the topiary, sieve 300g of the royal icing into a bowl; only add a little water as the mixture should be thick but workable. Add a few drops of the green food colouring. With the back of a fork smooth the icing onto the rounds of the lollipops, completely covering them and twisting as you go to make a textured surface. Sprinkle with edible glitter and leave to dry at room temperature, using orange halves as a stand by piercing the skin with the lollipop sticks. Once hard, mix up the remaining royal icing, split into halves and add red food colouring to one. Pipe each tree with either red or white roses.

To finish, pierce the topiary lollipop sticks into the centres of the cupcakes.

MAD HATTER CUPCAKE BOX

The Mad Hatter's top hat makes an ideal travelling box for delicate cupcakes, ensuring they get to the recipient looking pristine. If you don't get peckish on the journey, that is.

You will need
medium-weight card
assortment of patterned papers
PVA glue
craft knife
metal ruler
scissors
double-sided sticky tape
assortment of feathers, buttons
and ribbons, for decoration

~ trim the brim ~

~ score the paper ~

❧ To make the base of the box, cut a 13cm-diameter disc from the card. Using PVA glue, cover the card disc completely with patterned paper. Trim the edges neatly using a craft knife.

❧ Cut a 23cm x 4cm rectangle of patterned paper. Using a metal ruler and the blunt end of a pair of scissors or craft knife, score a fold line on the wrong side of the paper, 1cm in from one long edge.

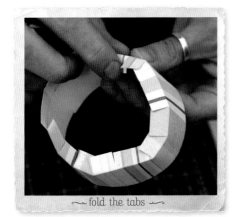

~ fold the tabs ~

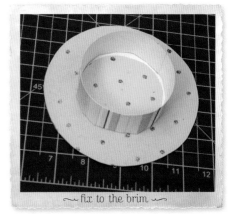

~ fix to the brim ~

❧ To make the tabs, cut a series of small snips, approximately 5mm apart, along the top edge of the paper up to – but not over – the fold line. Overlap the two short ends to make a tube and secure with double-sided sticky tape. Fold the cut tabs inwards.

❧ Using PVA glue, fix the tabs to the brim, making sure the tube is centrally positioned. Cut a 7.5cm-diameter disc from the same patterned paper used to cover the brim. Glue this small paper disc inside the tube to cover up the messy tabs.

continued

~ glue the crown ~

~ decorate and hide! ~

~ To make the crown, cut a 26cm x 8cm rectangle from patterned paper. Following the same method, make a tube with fold-over tabs as before.

~ Cut an 8cm-diameter disc from patterned paper. Glue to the tabs on the crown of the hat. Trim away any excess paper from the disc.

~ To make the hat band, cut a 26cm x 4cm strip from a contrasting paper. Wrap around the crown and fix with glue at the back and decorate with feathers, buttons and any trimmings you have spare. Allow to dry.

~ Once the glue is dry, carefully place a cupcake inside the brim of the hat and cover with the crown.

'Take off your hat,' the King said to the Hatter.

'It isn't mine,' said the Hatter.

'Stolen!' the King exclaimed, turning to the jury, who instantly made a memorandum of the fact.

'I keep them to sell,' the Hatter added as an explanation; 'I've none of my own. I'm a hatter.'

"'*Will you walk a little faster?*' said a whiting to a snail.
'*There's a porpoise close behind us, and he's treading on my tail.*
See how eagerly the lobsters and the turtles all advance!
They are waiting on the shingle – will you come and join the dance?
Will you, won't you, will you, won't you, will you join the dance?
Will you, won't you, will you, won't you,
won't you join the dance?'"

RED VELVET CUPCAKES

For the cakes
170g self-raising flour
½ teaspoon baking powder
pinch of salt
2 heaped tablespoon cocoa
30ml natural red food colouring
55g unsalted butter
170g caster sugar
1 large egg, beaten
1 teaspoon vanilla extract
120ml sour cream or buttermilk
½ teaspoon white vinegar
½ teaspoon baking soda

For the frosting
55g butter
120g full-fat cream cheese
170g icing sugar
1 teaspoon vanilla extract

Makes 12 cupcakes

Preheat the oven to 180°C/350°F/gas mark 4. Place 12 paper cases into a regular cupcake tin.

Sift the flour, baking powder and salt into a bowl and set aside. In a small bowl, combine the cocoa powder and food colouring; blend until thick and shiny with no lumps. Cream the butter and sugar together in a large bowl until light and fluffy. Slowly add the egg, then the cocoa paste and vanilla extract; mix until smooth. Add the sifted flour and the sour cream or buttermilk, stirring in alternate spoonfuls until the mixture is well blended. In a cup, mix the vinegar and baking soda; there will be a fizz! Combine this with the cake mixture.

Spoon the cake mixture into the paper cases, dividing it equally, and bake for 20 minutes. Allow the cakes to cool fully before adding the frosting.

To decorate: Combine the butter and cream cheese; blend until smooth. Sift in the icing sugar and add the vanilla extract. Using a large star-shaped nozzle, ice the cupcakes. Add crowns cut from gold paper using the template on page 136. If desired, make the crown strip longer, then cut hearts from the crown and add to the crown tips.

"Then followed the Knave of Hearts, carrying the King's crown on a crimson velvet cushion; and, last of all this grand procession, came the King and Queen of Hearts."

RED KING SLIPPERS

The Red King was a sleepy kind of fellow; his loud snores were often mistaken for thunder. These warm slippers are ideal for all the family, from babies to grannies, and they'll make you smile every time you look at their curly toes.

You will need

thick felt – the amount varies depending on the shoe size you are making; to fit an average-size child's foot, you will need 3 pieces of A4 felt
embroidery thread in contrasting colour
1m length of pompom trim (optional)
other pompoms or scraps of felt for trimmings

Note: If possible, try to get natural wool felt as it is much thicker and warmer than polyester felt.

~ join the heel ~

⮌ Using the templates on pages 128–129, cut the four uppers and two soles from felt. Hand sew the heel seam with blanket stitch.

~ stitch the toe ~

⮌ Again with blanket stitch, sew the uppers together at the front from the top, around the toe curl, down to the point marked "A".

~ attach the sole ~

⮌ To attach the sole, line up point "B" with the heel seam. Sew the sole in place with blanket stitch.

~ add some decoration ~

⮌ Decorate the slippers by adding felt shapes, pompom trim around the opening or large pompoms to the toes.

"It's only the Red King snoring,' said Tweedledee. 'Isn't he a lovely sight?' said Tweedledum. Alice couldn't say honestly that he was. He had a tall red night-cap on, with a tassel, and he was lying crumpled up into a sort of untidy heap, and snoring loud – fit to snore his head off!'"

TWEEDLEDUM & TWEEDLEDEE SHOEBAGS

These drawstring bags do a great job protecting your shoes.
They are almost the same but slightly different, just like their namesakes.

You will need per bag
offcuts of fabric, such as heavyweight cotton, denim and linen, for front panel
32cm x 26cm heavyweight fabric, for back panel
2 pieces, each 36cm x 26cm, of soft cotton, for lining
matching sewing thread
tailor's chalk or fading pen
two 80cm lengths of ribbon or cord
saftey pin
23cm x 13cm fabric, for drawstring hearts
ribbons, fine-cotton scraps, braids and buttons, for decoration

Note: The seam allowance is 1cm throughout.

To make the patchwork bag front, machine stitch together pieces of contrasting pattern fabrics to make a 32cm high x 26cm wide panel. For Dum's bag (top left) we joined eight 10cm high x 14cm wide patches. For Dee's bag (bottom right) we pieced together four 17cm high x 14cm wide patches.

Press open the seams then, if necessary, trim the panel down to 32cm x 26cm.

To join the front panel and lining, place together the patchwork panel and one lining piece with right sides facing. Pin and tack. Stitch along one short edge with a 1cm seam allowance. Repeat with the back panel and the remaining lining. Press open the seams.

Place together the front and back panels and the lining pieces with right sides facing. Make sure the main seams between the outer panels and the linings are aligned. Pin and tack.

With either tailor's chalk or a fading pen, on the lining mark parallel lines at 2cm and 4cm down from the main seam. This will be the drawstring channel.

Machine stitch the panels together, starting at the base of the lining, up to the first drawstring channel mark. Start stitching again after the other mark. Repeat on the other side. Leave a 10cm opening in the lining for the turning hole.

Turn the bag right sides out through the turning hole and press. Turn under the edges and hand sew the turning hole closed.

Ease the lining down into the outer bag until the bases touch. Approximately 2cm of the lining will be visible above the top edge of the outer bag. Press along this edge to make a firm crease in the lining.

To make a border, turn down the lining until the drawstring channels can be seen. Press. Topstitch along the border's lower edge.

drawstring channel

outer   lining   turning hole

drawstring channel

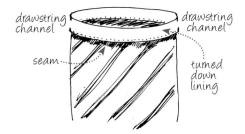

drawstring channel   drawstring channel

seam   turned down lining

SHOEBAGS {CONT}

👉 Attach a safety pin that is small enough to pass through the drawstring channel to one end of an 80cm length of ribbon or cord. Pass the safety pin and cord into the left-hand channel hole and thread it around the channel and back out of the same hole. Repeat with the other length of ribbon or cord and the right-hand hole.

To decorate
👉 Using the 5.5cm apron heart template on page 139, cut eight hearts with pinking shears from a print fabric. Sandwich one end of a drawstring between two hearts and stitch the hearts together around the edge. Repeat on the three other drawstring ends.

👉 Add any other decoration, such as lines of gold braid or letters and shapes made from narrow gold cord.

To make the rosette
👉 Rip or cut four 14cm x 2cm strips of fine cotton. Fold each of these strips into a loop. Place the loops one on top of each other in a star formation with raw ends together. Secure with a few stitches in the centre.

👉 Rip or cut a 40cm x 6cm strip of fine cotton. Sew a line of gathering stitches along one long edge. Pull each end of the thread to gather the strip into a circle. Gently flatten the gathers to create even pleats. Press into shape. Sew the two short edges of the strip together.

👉 Place the fabric star in the centre of the pleated circle. Secure with a few stitches in the centre. Use a large button to cover the join.

👉 Fold in half a 30cm length of 3cm-wide ribbon. Cut the ends into neat diagonal slants. Attach to the underside of the rosette. Secure the rosette to the shoebag with a few stitches.

"Tweedledum and Tweedledee agreed to have a battle!
For Tweedledum said Tweedledee had spoiled his nice new rattle.
Just then flew down a monstrous crow, as black as a tar-barrel!
Which frightened both the heroes so, they quite forgot their quarrel."

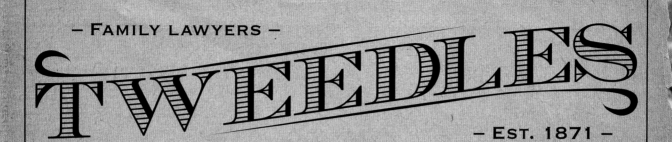

WONDERLAND APRONS

Create one of these stunning aprons to keep you neat and tidy in the kitchen whilst cooking a storm with our "Eat Me" recipes.

Alice's Apron

You will need
2.5m of 1.3m-wide (minimum) toile de jouy
2m x 10cm lightweight white cotton
matching sewing thread
3m length of 1cm-wide navy velvet ribbon
1m length of 1cm-wide white lace

Note: The seam allowance is 1cm throughout.

Using the template on page 138, cut two body pieces from the toile de jouy. Transfer any markings from the template to the fabric.

To make the apron, place the pieces together with right sides facing. Pin and tack. Stitch around the edges with a 1cm seam allowance, leaving between points "A" and "B" open. If necessary, clip the curved seams. Turn right sides out. Press. Turn under a 1cm hem along the open edge and topstitch closed.

For the neck strap, cut a strip of toile measuring 112cm x 12cm. Press under a 1cm hem on all edges, keeping them straight. Fold the strip in half lengthways with right sides facing out. Topstitch along all four sides.

To make the strap frill, fold the white cotton in half lengthways with right sides facing out. Press. Pin the strip along the neck strap in evenly spaced box pleats. One way to do this is to pin the middle and ends of the strip to the corresponding points on the strap, then work the pleats within these sections. Tack, then topstitch. Pin the neck strap to the top of the waistband at the marked points "X" and "Y". Pin and sew the strap to the apron with the frill on the outside edge.

For the waistband tie, cut a strip of toile measuring 242cm x 17cm. Make as for the neck strap. Fold the tie in half and mark the centre with a pin. Align this pin with marked point "C" on the apron. Pin in place across the waist and over the neck strap ends. Topstitch in place.

For the skirt frill, cut a strip of toile de jouy measuring 150cm x 16cm. Turn under a 1cm hem along both sides and the bottom edge. Trim with velvet ribbon. To make evenly spaced box pleats, pin the raw edge of the frill to the marked line "3" on the apron. Pin and tack, then topstitch. Cover the raw edge with a length of lace and velvet ribbon.

To finish, trim the bib of the apron with a length of lace and velvet ribbon as shown.

HOW TO BOX PLEAT

Fold the fabric so the two upper folds of the pleat face in opposite directions, while the two under folds are laid toward each other.

Queen of Hearts' Apron

You will need
2.5m of 1.3m-wide (minimum)
red polka dot cotton
matching sewing thread
4m length of 5cm-wide cream lace

Note: The seam allowance
is 1cm throughout.

⚬ Using the template on page 138, cut two body pieces from the cotton following the heart neckline. Transfer any markings.

⚬ To make the apron, place the pieces together with right sides facing. Pin and tack. Stitch around the edges with a 1cm seam allowance, leaving between points "A" and "B" open. Clip the corners and notch any curved seams. Turn right sides out. Press. Turn under a 1cm hem along the open V-shaped neckline and press.

⚬ For the neck strap, cut a strip of cotton measuring 112cm x 12cm. Make as for the method given for Alice's Apron on page 82. Sandwich one end of the neck strap between the apron at point "A". Pin in place. Repeat with the other end at point "B", making sure the strap does not twist. Topstitch along the neckline between points "A" and "B" to secure the strap and close the opening. Trim the outside edge of the apron body with lace.

⚬ For the waistband tie, cut a strip of cotton measuring 242cm x 17cm. Make as for the neck strap. Fold the tie in half and mark the centre with a pin. Align this pin with point "C" on the apron body. Pin the tie in place across the waist. Topstitch in place and trim the upper and lower edges with lace.

⚬ For the waistband tie ends, cut four small hearts from the cotton using the template on page 139. For each end, pin two hearts

together with right sides facing. Stitch together, leaving the top edge open for inserting the tie end. Clip the corners and notch any curved seams. Turn right sides out. Turn under a 1cm hem along the open edge and press. Insert one end of the tie into the heart. Pin in place. Repeat with the other end and the second heart. Topstitch to secure the hearts and close the opening. Trim the hearts with lace on both sides.

⚬ To make the pockets, cut four large hearts from the cotton using the template on page 139. For each pocket, pin two hearts together with right sides facing. Stitch together, leaving one side edge open. Clip the corners and notch any curved seams. Turn right sides out. Turn under a 1cm hem along the open edges and press. Topstitch to close the opening. Trim the hearts with lace on one side. Topstitch the pockets to the skirt of the apron, leaving the top open.

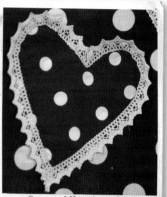

~ Queen of Heart's pocket ~

Cheshire Cat Apron

You will need

3m of 1.3-wide (minimum) striped
cotton ticking
matching sewing thread
20cm square of red felt
5.7m length of 2cm-wide black hemming
tape (can be iron-on for ease)

Note: The seam allowance
is 1cm throughout.

👉 Using the template on page 138, cut
two body pieces from the cotton ticking.
Transfer any markings.

👉 To make the apron, place the pieces
together with right sides facing. Pin and tack.
Stitch around the edges with a 1cm seam
allowance, leaving between points "A"
and "B" open. Clip the corners and notch
any curved seams. Turn right sides out. Press.
Turn under a 1cm hem along the neck edge
and press.

👉 For the neck strap, cut a strip of ticking
measuring 112cm x 12cm. Make as for
Alice's Apron on page 82. Sandwich one end
of the neck strap between the apron at point
"A". Pin in place. Repeat with the other end
at point "B", making sure the strap does not
twist. Topstitch along the neckline between

points "A" and "B" to secure the strap
and close the opening.

👉 To make the frills, cut three strips of
ticking measuring 150cm x 16cm. Turn
under a 1cm hem on the sides and lower
edges of the frills. Trim with black tape. Pin
the raw edge of one frill to the apron along
the marked line "3", making evenly spaced
box pleats. Tack, then topstitch down.
Repeat along lines "2" and "1", making sure
each frill overlaps the one below by 1cm.

👉 For the waistband tie, cut a strip of
ticking measuring 240cm x 17cm. Make as
for the neck strap. To attach the tie, follow
the method given for the Queen of Hearts'
Apron opposite, making sure the frills are
fully tucked beneath the waistband. Tack,
then topstitch down.

👉 To make the Cheshire Cat appliqué,
using the template on page 139, cut the cat
shape from red felt. Pin and tack the felt
shape to the upper right of the bib. Topstitch
in place, leaving the tail unstitched and free.

" 'I want a clean cup,' said the Hatter. 'Let's all move one place on.'

He moved on as he spoke, and the Dormouse followed him: the March Hare moved into the Dormouse's place, and Alice rather unwillingly took the place of the March Hare. The Hatter was the only one who got any advantage from the change: and Alice was a good deal worse off, as the March Hare had just upset the milk jug into his plate."

MUSICAL CHAIRS: AN INSTRUCTION
by the Mad Hatter

1 Place a number of chairs in a line. You must have one less chair than participants.

2 All participants must stand in a row in front of the chairs. When the music starts everyone must move around the chairs in a clockwise direction.

3 When the music stops all participants must try to sit on the chair closest to them. The player left without a chair is eliminated and one chair is also removed from the game.

4 Start and stop the music at varying intervals of time. Eliminate one participant and one chair each time.

5 Award a prize to the last remaining participant, that being the person sitting on the last chair.

TEA SET INVITATIONS

Every party needs invitations so why not make these simple and effective cards.
You could always try your hand at Looking-Glass writing for secret messages.

You will need per invitation
4 sheets of A1 patterned card
PVA glue
1 mini luggage tag (optional)
alphabet rubber stamps
or pen

For the envelope
watercolour paper
heart-shaped hole-punch

✎ Using the templates on page 130 and the patterned card, cut one teapot and the two teapot-base discs (small and medium); then cut one teacup, two saucer discs (small for the centre and large for the base) and a saucer rim piece. Cut one small connecting tab and one label per invitation.

✎ Glue the saucer rim and centre to the saucer base, and the teapot-base centre to the base. Fold the connecting tab in half. Glue half of the tab to the lower edge of the back of the teapot or teacup and the other half to the centre of the teapot base or saucer.

✎ Either by hand or with a small rubber stamp, write the type of celebration on the label (or luggage tag) – for example, birthday party, anniversary party, wedding – and your message on the back of the invitation.

✎ For the envelope, cut a square of watercolour paper big enough for your invite (test the size with scrap paper first) and fold each corner to the centre. Hole-punch a heart in the point of the bottom envelope flap. Cut a small scrap of patterned card and glue it behind the heart-shaped hole so the pattern shows through. Glue the envelope's bottom flap to the side flaps. Leave the top flap open so you can place the invitation card inside. When the invite is ready to be posted, simply glue down the top flap of the envelope or use a sticker to secure.

CROWN PLACECARDS

These crowns make delightful placecards, but they work equally well as quirky little party favours and unusual napkin holders.

Make these crowns in sophisticated creams and gold to add a touch of elegance to your dining table or use brightly patterned card for a children's fun party. You could just make the basic crown and then let your guests decorate them as a party activity; they make great going-home presents.

You will need per placecard
1 sheet of A4 thin card
ribbons, scraps of paper
and stick-on gemstones or
sequins for decoration
1 sheet of A4 patterned paper
alphabet rubber stamps
or pen
double-sided sticky tape
35cm length of thin
elasticated cord
1 paper napkin

☞ Using the templates on page 129, trace your chosen crown outline onto the reverse of the A4 card. Use a hard pencil so no marks are left on the card (although you can easily remove any marks with an eraser).

☞ Cut out the crown shape carefully with either a pair of scissors or a craft knife and cutting mat.

☞ Using a thick needle, pierce two holes in the crown where marked on the template.

☞ Now it's time to get creative! Decorate the crown with sequins, stick-on gemstones and ribbons. Personalise each crown to suit your individual guests.

☞ To make the nameplate, cut the shape from contrasting paper and adhere to the centre of the crown with glue or double-sided sticky tape. Add the name of your guest to the the nameplate either with rubber stamps or in pen in your finest handwriting.

☞ Fix a thin strip of double-sided sticky tape to the overlap edges of the crown. Join the edges and fix in place. Make sure the points of the crown line up.

☞ Tie a knot in one end of the elasticated cord. Thread the cord through one of the holes. Thread the other end of the cord through the second hole and tie another knot. If you want to fix the cord more firmly in place, use a square of sticky tape.

☞ To use the crown as a napkin holder, simply push a napkin inside the crown from beneath so it sits neatly inside.

" To the Looking-Glass world it was Alice that said
'I've a sceptre in hand, I've a crown on my head.
Let the Looking-Glass creatures, whatever they be
Come and dine with the Red Queen, the White Queen, and me!' "

VINTAGE CAKE STAND

"I love shopping for vintage tea sets; you can pick up some bargains from charity shops, yard sales and internet auctions sites. My favourite vintage brands are Shelly, Foley and Tuscan China." Hannah

You will need
4 plates in consecutively smaller sizes
4 small teacups, glasses or candlesticks
pen
ceramic glue or superglue

~ Play around with the layout of your cake stand before committing to glue the crockery together.

~ Find the central point on the base of each piece and mark the spot in pen. For each level, glue the corresponding plate to its connecting teacup, glass or candlestick, aligning the marks. Allow the glue to set. Working from the bottom up, join the glued sections together layer by layer.

~ To clean, always wash the cake stand gently by hand.

THE PERFECT AFTERNOON TEA

Afternoon tea is a perfect time for friends to get together for a good gossip and some tasty treats.

Setting the scene

Freshly ironed linens, sparkling silver and fine china are a must for a nicely turned out tea party. Make the centrepiece of the table a well-laden cake stand, while posies of fresh flowers add interest – but nothing too scented that will mask the smell of home-baked cakes and brewing tea. Keep flowers small and low so your guest's view is unobstructed. Lighting is all important at elegant soirees; candlelight or peach-coloured lightbulbs cast a flattering glow.

Filling the cake stand

On the first tier, place dainty finger sandwiches. On the second tier, small scones with cream and jams served in seperate bowls. An array of bite-size petit fours and pastries will complete your tea. Enjoy!

CHESHIRE CAT SANDWICHES

Watch your very own Cheshire Cat disappear before your eyes as your guests delve into these delicious stripy sandwiches!

You will need

1 loaf of medium-sliced white bread
1 loaf of medium sliced brown bread
butter
sandwich filling of your choice

☞ Butter the white and brown loaves. To make the striped bread, place alternate white and brown slices on top of each other. We layered four slices in a block; each of these blocks makes two sandwiches made up of three-layers.

☞ Push the slices of bread down gently and evenly, then wrap tightly in clingfilm and freeze for a few hours.

☞ Remove the bread from the freezer and allow to defrost for approximately 30 minutes. Slice downwards with a sharp breadknife – much like a normal loaf – through the layers in 1cm slices to reveal your stripy bread. Neaten the slices at each end by trimming the crusts. Add your favourite sandwich filling.

SANDWICH TOPPERS

Copy this page and mount it onto card. Cut out each shape, then glue or tape each one to a cocktail stick to make a topper.

WONDERLAND COOKIE CUTTERS

Although there are plenty of interesting shaped cookie cutters available, it's always good to be able to make something completely unique for a special occasion. With this method, cutters are simple to make and in almost any shape imaginable.

You will need
disposable aluminium baking trays
(ones with long straight edges are best)
metal ruler
old scissors or tin snips
protective gloves

~ remove the straight sides ~

~ score the overlapped sides ~

↬ Wearing gloves to protect your hands, cut the straight sides from the baking tray. Flatten them out as much as possible. To make a 10cm diameter heart cutter you need approximately a 40cm length of these straight sides.

↬ Lay all the flat aluminium pieces together in a long line, overlapping each end by approximately 1cm. Using the metal rule and scissors, score a straight line along the long edge approximately 1cm in from the rim.

~ press the rim down flat ~

~ shape the cookie cutter ~

~ the finished cutters ~

↬ Fold the rim inwards along the scored line and, using closed scissors, press the aluminium down as flat as possible. This locks the strip together.

↬ Gently bend the aluminium strip into your required shape. Join the cutter by slotting one end of the strip into the other. Press together firmly.

↬ Using your fingers and thumbs, smooth out any bends and corners in the cutters to perfect the shape – teacup, mushroom or pocket watch!

HOW TO "FLOOD" ICE

✏ Flood icing gives a lovely smooth surface to a cookie. It is a very satisfying way of decorating cookies and achieving a professional finish.

You will need
royal icing sugar
small amount of water
selection of food colourings
piping bags with small round nozzles
squeezy condiment bottles

1 Mix a small amount of the royal icing sugar with a few drops of water to make a smooth consistency that forms soft peaks. The icing needs to be just stiff enough to keep its shape when piped. Divide the icing into small bowls – one for each colour you wish to use – then add the food colouring and mix well.

2 Using a piping bag with a small round nozzle, pipe the outline of each seperate coloured area onto your cookies. Allow to dry for a few minutes.

3 Mix a little more royal icing sugar with a few more drops of water to create a runny icing that drips off your spoon. Mix in the food colouring then place in a piping bag (or if you can find them, a plastic condiment bottle as they are less messy and easier to clean). Fill each outlined area with the colour to match in zigzags. It's okay to ice three or four cookies at a time as the icing takes a while to dry.

4 Using a cocktail stick, move the icing around to fill any little holes and create a flat surface. Allow to dry – ideally overnight – in a cool place. If you wish to add any extra details or further flourishes to your decoration, use soft-peak icing and a fine nozzle or the excellent ready-made decorating tubes.

WONDERLAND COOKIES

Too many of these magical mushroom cookies might possibly make you grow bigger.

You will need
250g unsalted butter
250g caster sugar
1 teaspoon vanilla extract
1 egg, lightly beaten
500g plain flour

 Cream together the butter, sugar and vanilla extract in a bowl until light and fluffy. Don't overmix, though, or your cookies may spread in the oven.

 Add the egg and gently mix. Add the flour gradually and mix well. The dough is ready when it forms a single lump in the bottom of the bowl and no crumbs are left.

 Wrap the dough in clingfilm and chill in the fridge for at least 1 hour. (Alternatively, you can freeze the dough for up to one month for use at a later date.) Preheat the oven to 180°C/gas mark 4.

 Place the dough on a floured surface. Roll out the dough to an even thickness of approximately 4mm. Using your cookie cutters, press out the cookie shapes. With a palette knife, transfer to a greaseproof paper-lined baking tray. Chill for a further 30 minutes.

 Bake for 10–12 minutes until the cookies are golden brown. Allow to cool completely on a wire rack.

 How long your cookies last will depend on the appetite of who you've made them for! But un-iced, they should last for up to one month in an airtight box.

JAM POT TOPPERS

You will need
oddments of fabric,
twice the diameter of the
lids on your jam jars
elastic bands
a selection of ribbons
and other trims
sticky labels

☞ Cut a disc of fabric twice
the diameter of your jam-jar lid
(ie. for an 8cm lid, cut a 16cm
disc). Trim the disc with lace
or bias binding, or cut a zigzag
edge with pinking shears.

☞ Place the disc centrally
over the lid and secure with an
elastic band. Tie a ribbon over
the elastic band to hide it.
On a sticky label, write the
date and flavour of jam.

PRETTY PRESERVES

Red Rose Petal Jam

This jam has a distinct floral flavour, combining notes of strawberry with citrus.

You will need
230g edible red rose petals
460g caster sugar
juice of 2 lemons
few drops of rosewater

Makes 5 medium jars

Place the petals in a colander and rinse them under a tap. Remove the stems and any discoloured petals. Place in a large bowl and cover with water. Place a smaller plate on top of the petals to weigh them down.

Soak at room temperature for at least 1 hour (this can be done for up to 3 days).

Drain the petals and pat dry with kitchen towel or whiz in a salad spinner. Bruise the petals slightly with your hands and place them back into a bowl. Add a few drops of rosewater to taste. Sprinkle the petals with one third of the sugar and lightly toss to coat evenly. Cover the bowl with clingfilm and leave overnight to infuse.

In a deep saucepan, bring 1 litre of water to the boil. Add the lemon juice and remaining two thirds of the sugar. Stir in the petals with a wooden spoon and simmer for 30 minutes.

Bring the mixture back to the boil for 15–20 minutes, until the jam has thickened. Remove any froth as it boils. To test if the jam has set, spoon a small amount on to a plate and place in the fridge for one

minute. If it forms a skin, the jam is ready. If it is still runny, boil the jam and test it every 3 minutes. Allow the jam to cool in the pan for 10 minutes.

To sterilise the jam jars, boil them in water. Pour the jam into the jars, seal and allow to cool. Take care as the jars will be very hot.

Spread onto some crusty white bread or a croissant with some unsalted butter. Yum!

Merry King Marmalade

Why not spread this fragrant citrus treat on top of some warmed teacakes? Perfect for breakfast.

You will need
6–8 small oranges
juice of 1 lemon
1.1kg granulated sugar

Makes 5 medium jars

Slice the oranges in half and squeeze out their juice. Scoop out any remaining flesh from the oranges and whiz in a blender. Sieve into

a deep saucepan along with the juice. Remove any pith from the orange halves. Slice the rind into thin matchsticks.

Add the lemon juice, rind matchsticks and 1.4 litres of water to the orange juice in the pan. Bring to the boil then simmer for 1½ hours. Remove any froth as it boils. At this stage, for a

clear marmalade remove the pieces of rind.

Add the sugar and stir well until dissolved. Boil for a further 10–15 minutes or until thickened; remove any more froth as necessary. To test if the marmalade has set, spoon a small amount on to a plate and place in the fridge for one minute. If it

forms a skin, the marmalade is ready. If it is still runny, boil and test it every 3 minutes. Allow the marmalade to cool in the pan for 10 minutes.

To sterilise the jam jars, boil them in water. Pour the jam into the jars, seal and allow to cool. Take care as the jars will be very hot.

"She took down a jar from one of the shelves as she passed; it was labelled

ORANGE MARMALADE

but to her great disappointment it was empty."

MARCH HARE'S HOUSE TEACOSY

Make teatime extra special with this spin on the classic "house" teacosy.
Be careful not to gossip too much over your cuppa as he is listening!

You will need

1m x 1m beige cotton twill
50cm x 50cm of 2cm-thick cotton wadding
50cm x 20cm floral print cotton
50cm x 20cm white felt
small 10cm scraps of contrasting floral print cottons for windows, doors and curtains
30cm length of pompom trim
80cm length of lace

Note: The seam allowance is 1cm throughout.

Using the templates on page 133, cut two basic house pieces for the front and back of the teacosy from cotton twill. Cut two roof pieces from floral print cotton. Cut four window pieces from the scrap floral print cotton. Cut one door piece, one door arch and one heart all from scrap floral print cotton.

Stitch one roof piece to each of the basic house pieces. Using zigzag stitch, stitch two window pieces to the each of the house pieces, then stitch the door, arch and heart pieces to the front only. Zigzag stitch across the windows in both directions for the window panes. Zigzag stitch "cake slice" sections on the door arch for the window panes. Attach a length of pompom trim along the top of each window and a length of lace along the lower edge of the roof.

Using the templates on page 133, cut two basic house pieces from cotton wadding. Cut two inner teacosy pieces from the cotton twill. To each inner teacosy piece pin the decorated front and back of the house with right sides facing. Stitch around the curve leaving the straight lower edge free. Turn the right side out and stuff each with wadding. Turn over a double hem on the inner teacosy lining so that it sits on the outer side. Pin in place then topstitch to hem.

Using the templates on page 133, cut two outer ears from white felt and two inner ears from scrap floral print cotton. Zigzag stitch the inner ears onto the outer ears. Pinch at the bottom so inner ear is facing inwards and pin upside down to front of house (so that the ends are facing upwards).

To finish, tack both front and back together along the curve with right sides facing, making sure the roof lines align. Stitch together. Turn right side out and your teacosy is ready for its first pot of tea!

"She came in sight of the house of the March Hare: she thought it must be the right house, because the chimneys were shaped like ears and the roof was thatched with fur."

AFTERNOON TEAS

*There is nothing more relaxing than a cuppa, but why not spice
your tea up a little with these aromatic combinations.*

Each mix makes around 100g tea, providing you use heaped tablespoons. Simply throw all the ingredients into a bowl and mix. Store in an airtight container or decant into pretty presentation bags and tie with ribbon. Photocopy "The Perfect Cup of Tea" instructional and present it with the tea as a gift.

Black & Blue Tea

5 tablespoons dried cornflower petals
2 tablespoons dried lemon rind
8 tablespoons loose-leaf Earl Grey tea

Cornflower is not only aesthetically stunning with its bright blue petals, but it also holds great health benefits: it is an anti-inflammatory and it improves digestion.

English Rose Tea

5 tablespoons dried red rosebuds
2 tablespoons dried orange rind
8 tablespoons loose-leaf part black tea

This soothing aromatic tea has many traditional medicinal benefits; it is full of antioxidants and vitamin C, which cleanse the body and help with natural defences.

Sunflower Petal Tea

5 tablespoons dried sunflower petals
10 tablespoons loose-leaf part black tea
1 cinnamon stick

Reminiscent of summer on a chilly day, the rich, sweet honey aroma of sunflower petals with spicy cinnamon adds a sumptuous note to any black tea.

A SERIES OF INSTRUCTIONALS no. 2

THE PERFECT CUP OF TEA

It is traditional to use a teapot whilst making tea; it allows the tea time to infuse thus giving a fuller flavour.

You will need
Teapot • Tea Strainer
Teapot Cosy (optional)
Cups & Saucers

Fill the kettle with cold fresh water and boil. It is important not to re-boil water as it decreases its oxygen content making the tea less flavorful.

Warm the teapot with a splash of the boiled water and swirl around.

It is usual to add two teaspoons of tea per cup plus one for the pot.

Add boiling water and leave to steep for 3–4 minutes.

Strain into a cup and enjoy!

BEADED NAPKIN RINGS

Making an initial napkin ring for each of your guests gives your tea party a truly personal touch, they also double as delightful party favours.

You will need

2 pairs round nose pliers
wire cutters
3mm glass or plastic beads
1.5mm gauge silver-plated wire
0.8mm gauge silver-plated wire
0.6mm gauge silver-plated wire
cardboard tube, such as a toilet
roll inner tube

For the napkin ring

☞ Cut an 80cm length of 1.5mm gauge wire. Wrap the wire around a cardboard tube approximately four times to form a loosely wound coil. Slip the wire coil off of the cardboard tube. Pull the two ends of the wire towards each other to tighten the coil.

☞ Separate one end of the wire slightly from the coil; wrap this separated end around the entire coil to secure, making sure the other end is enclosed. You may find it easier to use round nose pliers to pull the wrapped wire end tight. Gently shape the coil in one hand to form an oval.

~ the back of the ring ~

For the decoration

☞ To make the beaded decoration, cut a 35cm length of 0.8mm gauge wire. Depending on the intricacy of your chosen initial letter, you may need a slightly longer length of wire.

☞ Using two pairs of round nose pliers, form a small loop at one end of the wire – hold the wire with one pair of pliers and form a loop with the other – to stop the beads from falling off. Thread the wire with your chosen beads. When the wire is fully threaded with beads, make another small loop in the same way. A little space between the beads for movement is preferable.

☞ Referring to the templates on page 131 for inspiration, bend the beaded wire into your chosen shape. If you prefer to form a heart rather than an initial, bend the beaded wire in the middle so that the two halves overlap then gently form each end into a heart. Continue moulding the wire until you find a shape that pleases you.

☞ To fix the beaded decoration to the napkin ring, cut a 25cm length of 0.6mm gauge wire. With the coil join to the back, wind the wire neatly around the front of the napkin ring and then once over the decoration (between two beads) and back around the napkin ring. Repeat wherever the decoration comes into contact with the napkin ring. Trim all the wire ends and tuck them in for safety.

~ Beaded Heart Napkin Ring ~

DUCHESS MACAROONS

*These exquisite rosewater and crushed lavender crème macaroons
are so scrumptious they are good enough for any royal!*

For the rose macaroons
175g icing sugar
125g ground almonds
1 teaspoon cream of tartar
3 large free-range egg whites,
at room temperature
a pinch of salt
75g caster sugar
a few drops of pink food
colouring
2 teaspoons rosewater

For the lavender crème
30g unsalted butter
70g cream cheese
100g icing sugar
4 heads of fresh edible
lavender flowers

To decorate
edible crystallised flowers

Makes 20+ macaroons

Preheat the oven to 160°C/gas mark 3.
Line two baking sheets with baking parchment.

In a food processor, grind the icing
sugar, almonds and cream of tartar to a fine
dust – this will take at least 3 minutes.

In a large bowl, whisk the egg whites
with a pinch of salt until they thicken and
form soft peaks – or until you are able to hold
the bowl upside down above your head
without them falling! Sift the caster sugar
into the egg whites a spoonful at a time. With
each addition, slowly whisk the sugar in until
the mixture is thick and glossy. Add 2 or 3
drops of pink food colouring along with the
rosewater and stir to combine.

Sift half the icing sugar mixture into
the egg whites. Using a spatula, gently
fold the two together until smooth.
Repeat with the remaining icing sugar
mixture, taking care not to overwork it.
The resulting macaroon mixture should
have a ribbon-like consistency.

Spoon the mixture into a piping bag
and pipe small rounds – each around 2cm
wide – onto your prepared baking sheets.
It is best to use a plain 1cm-wide nozzle
and, when piping, simply squeeze the bag
while holding the nozzle still. Make sure you
leave a 3cm space between each macaroon as
they will expand slightly in the oven.

Leave your macaroons to set at room
temperature for 15 minutes before baking:
it is very important they form a skin before

going into the oven. Bake for 10–12 minutes,
then remove from the oven.

Leave to cool on the baking sheet for
10–15 minutes – the macaroons are ready
to move only when the hard outer shell has
formed. Remove the macaroons from the
baking parchment – they will be sticky
underneath so take care; you may find it
easier to use a pallet knife – and place flat
side down onto a cooling rack.

To make the crushed lavender crème: Combine
the butter with the cream cheese in a bowl,
making sure it is well mixed. Sift the icing
sugar into the mixture and blend well.

Using a pestle and mortar, gently crush
the small lavender flowers and then fold them
into the crème. Cover the bowl and allow
the mixture to infuse for 1 or 2 hours (for a
stronger flavour, leave the mixture overnight).

To assemble: Dollop a teaspoon of the
lavender-infused crème onto half of the
cooled macaroon shells and then sandwich
each together with a second shell. Add the
finishing touch by decorating each macaroon
with an edible crystallised flower.

*Sit back with a cup of tea and enjoy a little piece
of macaroon heaven!*

PLAYING CARD BUNTING

This wonderful bunting is easy to make and it is very effective. The textured card
gives a wooden effect as well as waterproofing, perfect for outdoors.

You will need
2 sheets of white A2
mount board
black, white and red
acrylic paint
PVA glue
wide paintbrush
1 sheet of thin A4 card,
for stencil
hole-punch
10m length of 5cm-wide
red ribbon

Makes 4m of bunting

Using the templates on page 139, cut four hearts, diamonds, clubs, spades and playing-card shapes.

In three separate pots – one for each colour – mix one part acrylic paint to one part PVA glue. The red paint is for the hearts and diamonds, the black paint is for the clubs and spades while the white paint is for the playing cards. Lay the card shapes out on sheets of newspaper. With a wide paintbrush dab paint onto one side of the card shape so it has a raised effect. Allow to dry. Repeat this process on other side. For even more texture, repeat this process if desired.

Using the templates on page 139, make the two stencils from the thin card. With contrasting colour paint and using the stencils, dab the paint on to the diamonds and playing-card shapes. Allow to dry.

With a hole-punch, make a hole in the centre of each club, diamond and spade card shape, approximately 2cm from the top. Make two holes in each heart and playing-card shape, one on either side.

Cut a 4m length of ribbon and hang this where you want the bunting, such as outdoors for a garden party. Cut a shorter length of ribbon for each card shape. Thread each shape on to ribbon and tie them securely to the longer ribbon in a bow.

" "Who cares for you?" said Alice,
'You're nothing but a pack of cards!' "

CURIOUS TEAPOT CAKE

Create this fabulous centrepiece for your tea party; it makes a great talking point and is almost too good to eat! The teapot shape is formed from a microwaved sponge cake cooked in an ovenproof mixing bowl.

For the cake
1 pre-cooked small sponge pudding, Christmas pudding or microwaved sponge cake made in a 2 litre ovenproof bowl

For the icing
1 pack of ready-rolled marzipan
1 pack of ready-rolled icing
apricot jam
450g icing sugar, sifted
pink, green and blue food colouring
disposable piping bags and nozzles
fine paintbrush

For the decoration
2 blocks of white polymer modelling clay
1 box of toothpicks

~ mould the clay handle ~

~ mould the clay spout ~

Warm the clay in your hands so it is workable. To make the teapot handle, roll the clay into a 15cm long sausage approximately 1cm wide. Flatten the sausage, then roll each end inwards to form a spiral. Mould into a handle shape with the spirals facing inwards. Pierce each spiral end with a toothpick.

To make the teapot spout, work the clay into a slight cone shape approximately 10cm long. Mould into an "S" shape. With a sharp knife, cut across the top to form the spout hole and along the lower edge that will connect to the teapot. Pierce the lower flat edge with two toothpicks.

~ insert the cocktail sticks ~

~ bake the clay shapes ~

To make the teapot lid bobble, roll a ball approximately 2cm in diameter. Pierce with a toothpick.

Place on a tray and bake in the oven following the manufacturer's instructions. Once hardened, allow to cool.

continued

~ cover the teapot cake ~

~ cut out the teapot lid ~

~ assemble the teapot ~

✎ To decorate the cake, place the pre-cooked sponge onto a flat serving plate or board. Using a pastry brush, coat the surface of the cake with apricot jam. Smooth the ready-rolled marzipan onto the cake, covering it completely. Trim any excess from the lower edge to neaten. Repeat with the ready-rolled icing. Keep all the trimmings of icing for the next step.

✎ To make the teapot lid, roll the remaining icing out to approximately 2cm thick on a surface lightly dusted with icing sugar. Cut a 6cm disc from the icing – if you don't have a pastry cutter the correct size, use the rim of a teacup or glass.

✎ Coat one side of the teapot lid with apricot jam and place on top of iced teapot cake. Next, attach the baked clay teapot handle, spout and lid bobble by pushing the toothpicks into the cake.

~ pipe the iced flowers ~

~ blend the icing ~

~ taa-daaah! ~

✎ Mix up the icing in a bowl following the packet instructions. Divide the icing equally into four small bowls and add food colouring to three, leaving one white. With a piping bag and a 2mm round nozzle, pipe the flower and leaf decoration on to the teapot.

✎ For a more professional look, wet a fine paintbrush and blend the different icing colours into one another.

✎ Serve the finished teapot cake on the plate or board or, alternatively, transfer it carefully to a small cake stand. The perfect centrepiece for any Mad Tea Party!

CHOCOLATE TEASPOONS

The only thing as pointless as a chocolate teapot is a chocolate teaspoon!

You will need
milk or plain chocolate, glass bowl, saucepan which the bowl is slightly too big to fit into, a selection of teaspoons, edible silver, coins

🍫 Break the chocolate into small pieces and place into the glass bowl.

🍫 Fill the saucepan with a small amount water and balance the glass bowl on the rim of the pan. Place over a low heat and stir until the chocolate is melted. Do not allow the chocolate to boil or come into contact with the water.

🍫 To ensure the chocolate sets flat in the spoon bowls, prop the handles up on stacks of coins until level. Carefully fill the spoons with chocolate. Allow to set and then decorate with the edible silver. Stir into coffee, hot milk or drinking chocolate for an indulgent treat.

MAD HATTER HATS

If you've a wedding, garden, mad or fancy dress party to attend, one of these hats is sure to get you noticed.

For a Mad Hatter's tea party, one must be modelling the very latest head gear! Why not try your hand at making one of our designs?

We used contemporary materials mixed with the traditional – such as sinamay, a brightly coloured starched gauze, which comes in

pliable strips and hat bases. The wonderful thing about millinery is that anything goes. Especially when you are a Mad Hatter!

Flamingo Headpiece

You will need

1.5m length of 3cm-wide sinamay
bias binding
invisible thread
teardrop base sinamay headpiece in pink
30-piece fan of flamingo feathers

☞ To make the loops, bend the first
10cm of the sinamay bias binding into
an elongated loop. Stitch securely with
invisible thread. Do not cut. Repeat
with the next 20cm of the binding for
the concertina effect. Repeat a further
three times, each time adding another
10cm to the loop.

☞ Fix the loops to the headpiece
with a line of stitches along the lower
edge of the longest loop. Stitch securely
in place at the front.

☞ Split the fan of feathers into
groups of five. Place them between
each loop, then sew in place.

Cup & Saucer Hat

You will need

10–12cm plastic plant pot
50cm x 50cm toile de jouy
PVA glue
1 sheet of thick A4 card
gold spray paint
old teaspoon
1m length of 3mm gold rope trim
round base sinamay headpiece in cream

☞ To cover the plant pot, place a pen
mark on the inside rim of the pot. Make
a snip in the fabric and lie the pot
on its side so the pen mark
lines up with the snip. Roll the
pot along the fabric until it has
done a full rotation. Make
another snip. Adding a 2cm
seam allowance on all sides, cut
out the slightly curved rectangle
between snips. Clip and notch the
seam allowance at 1cm intervals.

Pour a little PVA glue into a pot and soften with a dash of water. Paint the glue onto the wrong side of the fabric rectangle and smooth onto the plant pot. Trim the overlapping side seam to neaten. Turn the seam allowances over at the rim and base.

To cover the inside of the pot, cut small strips of fabric to the height of the pot. Glue the strips neatly to the inside of the pot. For the inner base lining, trace around the pot's base and cut out a fabric disc. Glue the fabric disc to the inside base for a neat finish.

To make the saucer, cut a 16cm disc from the card. Cut a 20cm disc from the fabric. Glue the card to the centre of the fabric. Clip and notch the 2cm seam allowance and take over to the back of the card disc. Glue in place. Allow to dry thoroughly.

Cut a teacup handle from the card and spray with gold paint. Spray the teaspoon with gold paint. Allow to dry.

With a hot glue-gun, fix the teacup to the saucer then attach the handle. Glue the spoon to the saucer. Decorate with the gold rope trim. Glue the cup and saucer at an angle to the headpiece.

White Rabbit Ears

You will need
2m length of thick silver garden wire
1m x 50cm white satin
20mm pearlescent beads
wide sinamay headband in pink

To make the frame, twist together the ends of the wire to form one large loop. Trim any sharp ends. Keeping the wire flat, pinch the middle together. Mould each side into an ear, forming two petal shapes in a figure of eight.

Fold the fabric in half with wrong sides facing. Sandwich the wire frame in between the fabric. Pin in place. Trim any excess fabric along the open edges, leaving a 3cm seam allowance. Tuck in the seam allowance and pin – stretch the fabric taut but do not pull the frame out of shape. Machine stitch around the outer edges.

To attach the ears to the headband, fold the ears in half at the central point so both are facing foward. Feed the headband in between and wrap the back ear around the front ear to make a knot. Check that the ears are securely fixed and will not move around when worn. Curve the ear tips inwards.

For the pearl decoration, cut a 20cm length of wire and thread on the pearlescent beads. Tuck into the ear knot and twist the ends of the wire together. Trim any sharp ends.

Playing Card Hat

You will need
thick wool felt: 20cm square in each of red and white, and 20cm x 30cm piece in black
wide black hairband
28cm length of thick wire

 Cut out the felt shapes in varying sizes (4–6cm). Cut two hearts and two diamonds from red felt, two spades and one small and one large club from black felt, and one card shape from white felt.

Glue the small club to the card shape. Mould a semi-circle shape out of the wire and glue the ends slightly to one side of the hairband using a hot glue-gun. Attach the shapes with a slight overlap onto the wire. To finish, cut a 1cm x 30cm strip of black felt and glue to the back of the wire, gluing 1cm at each end to the hairband.

White Rose Hat

You will need
clear plastic haircomb
20 circles 24cm in diameter and 25 circles 20cm in diameter, all cut from various white and cream fabrics (such as stiff netting, silk, gauze and satins)
8cm felt disc
spray starch

Fold each of the small and large circles into quarters and trim the curved edges into heart shapes. Unfold and place the large circles one on top of another in sets of five, alternating the fabrics and colours. Don't worry about lining them up too neatly. Repeat with the small circles. You will now have five sets of small circles and four sets of large circles.

Fold each set of five into quarters and sew a few stitches at the point to secure the circles together.

Take the disc of felt and sew the four larger petal quarters to its centre, creating a circle. On top of this sew four of the five smaller petal quarters, staggering the first quarter so the top and bottom set don't line up.

Sew the fifth petal quarter into the centre of the rose. To plump up the rose, separate each set of petals by pulling individual petals away from each other. For extra stiffness spray the rose with the starch and iron individual tips.

Stitch the haircomb into place on the felt disc and wear with pride.

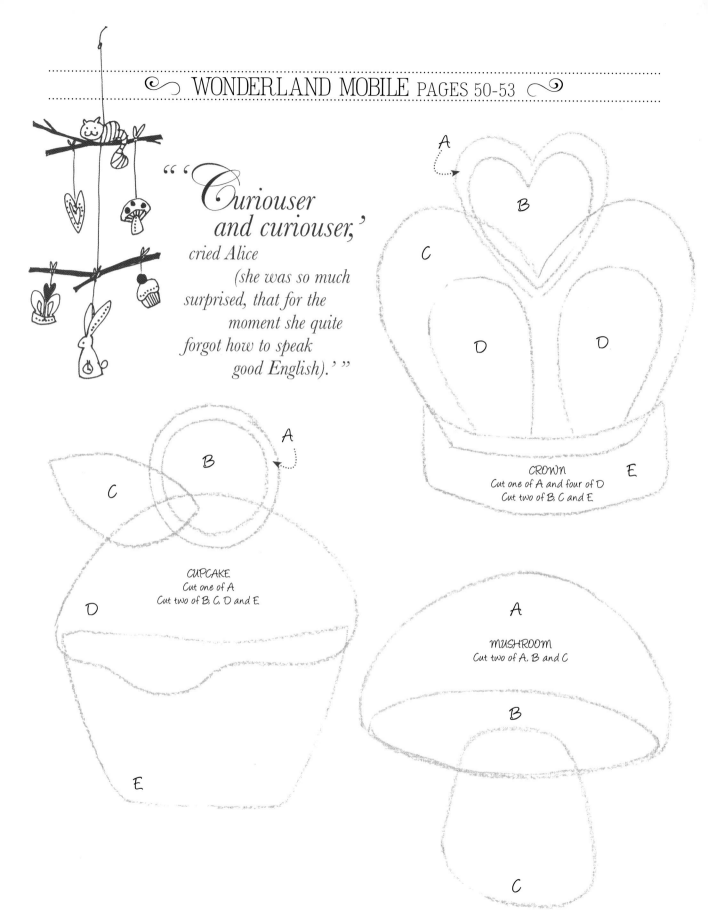

"'Curiouser and curiouser,' cried Alice *(she was so much surprised, that for the moment she quite forgot how to speak good English).'"*

A

B

C

D   D

CROWN
Cut one of A and four of D
Cut two of B, C and E

E

A

B

C

CUPCAKE
Cut one of A
Cut two of B, C, D and E

D

E

A

MUSHROOM
Cut two of A, B and C

B

C

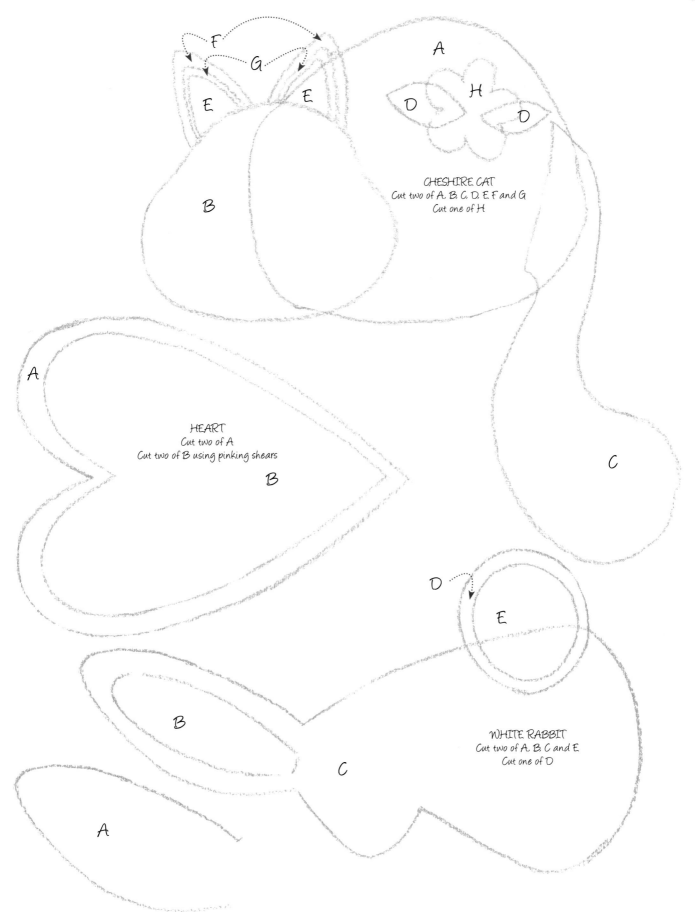

F

G

E

A

D H D

E

CHESHIRE CAT
Cut two of A, B, C, D, E, F and G
Cut one of H

A

HEART
Cut two of A
Cut two of B using pinking shears

B

C

D

E

B

C

WHITE RABBIT
Cut two of A, B, C and E
Cut one of D

A

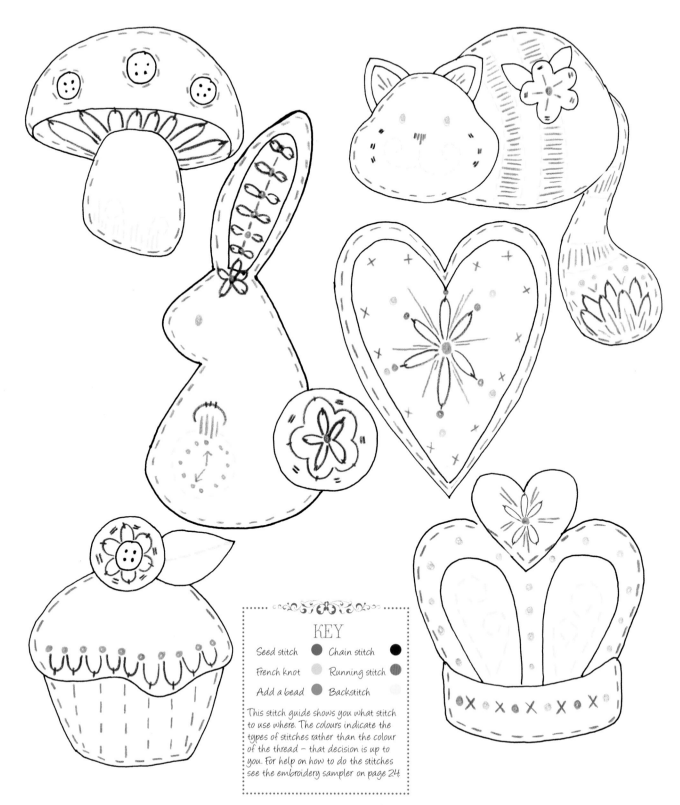

KEY

Seed stitch ●   Chain stitch ●

French knot ●   Running stitch ●

Add a bead ●   Backstitch ●

This stitch guide shows you what stitch to use where. The colours indicate the types of stitches rather than the colour of the thread – that decision is up to you. For help on how to do the stitches see the embroidery sampler on page 24.

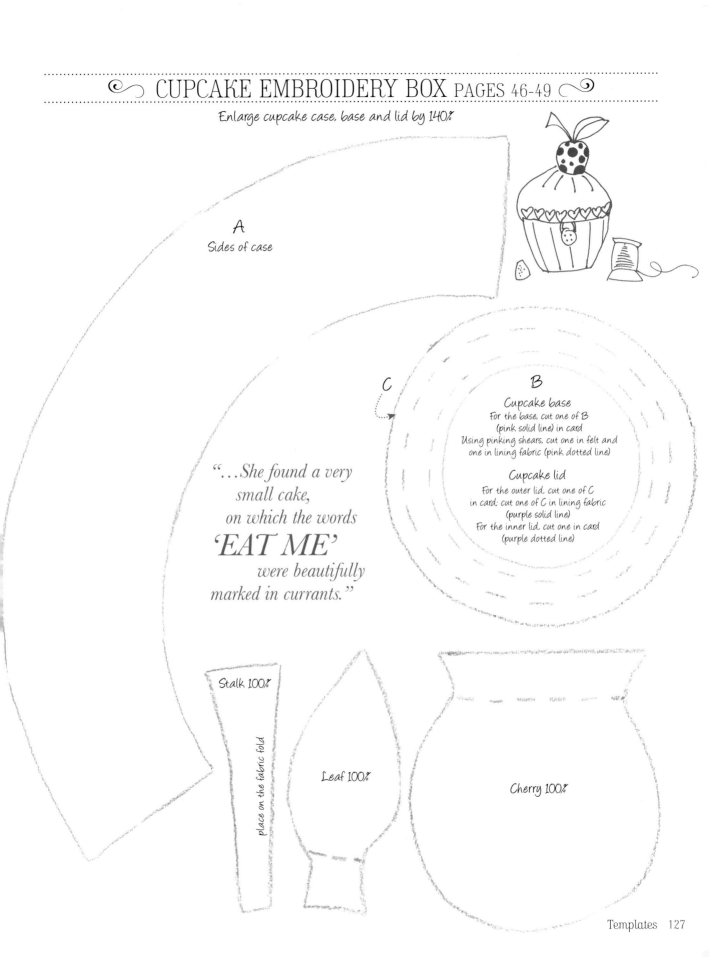

Enlarge cupcake case, base and lid by 140%

A

Sides of case

C

B

Cupcake base
For the base, cut one of B
(pink solid line) in card
Using pinking shears, cut one in felt and
one in lining fabric (pink dotted line)

Cupcake lid
For the outer lid, cut one of C
in card; cut one of C in lining fabric
(purple solid line)
For the inner lid, cut one in card
(purple dotted line)

"...She found a very
small cake,
on which the words
'EAT ME'
were beautifully
marked in currants."

Stalk 100%

place on the fabric fold

Leaf 100%

Cherry 100%

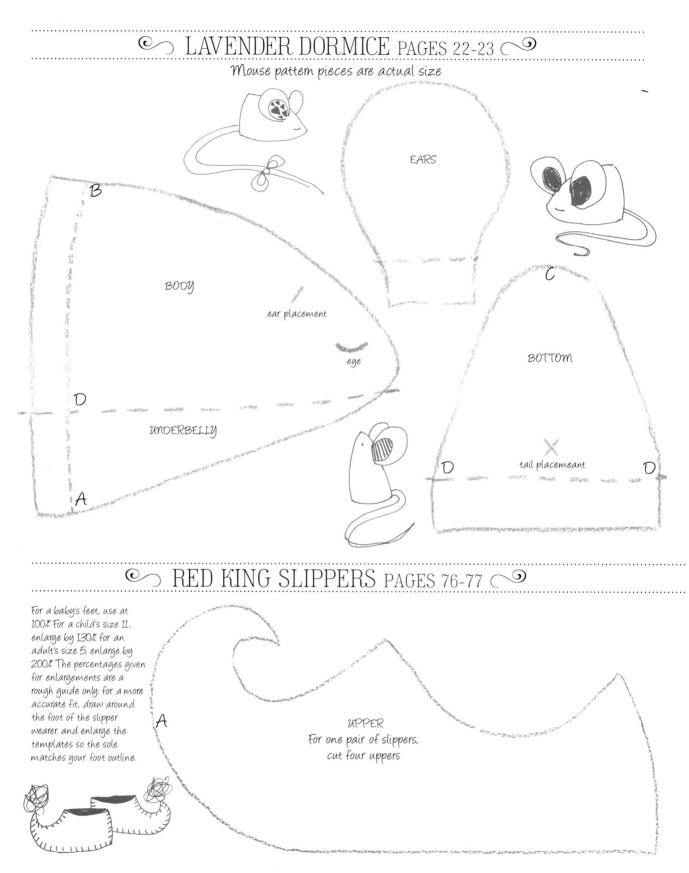

❧ LAVENDER DORMICE PAGES 22-23 ❧

Mouse pattern pieces are actual size

EARS

B

BODY

ear placement

eye

C

BOTTOM

D

UNDERBELLY

A

D   tail placemeant   D

❧ RED KING SLIPPERS PAGES 76-77 ❧

For a baby's feet, use at 100%. For a child's size 11, enlarge by 130%; for an adult's size 5, enlarge by 200%. The percentages given for enlargements are a rough guide only: for a more accurate fit, draw around the foot of the slipper wearer and enlarge the templates so the sole matches your foot outline.

A

UPPER
For one pair of slippers,
cut four uppers

CROWN PLACECARDS PAGE 90-91

Enlarge each crown shape by 140% to fit onto a sheet of A4 card

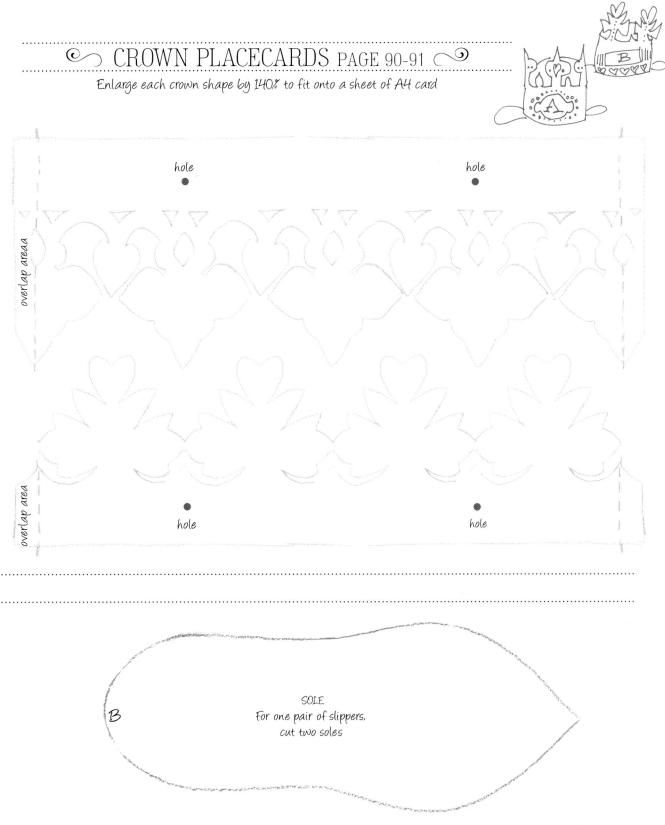

hole

hole

overlap area

overlap area

hole

hole

B

SOLE
For one pair of slippers,
cut two soles

"It's only the Red King snoring"

Enlarge templates by 130%

"*It's always tea-time,*
and we've no time to wash
the things between whiles,'
said the Hatter with a sigh."

SAUCER

LABEL

TEACUP

TEAPOT

TEAPOT
BASE

Enlarge template by 120%

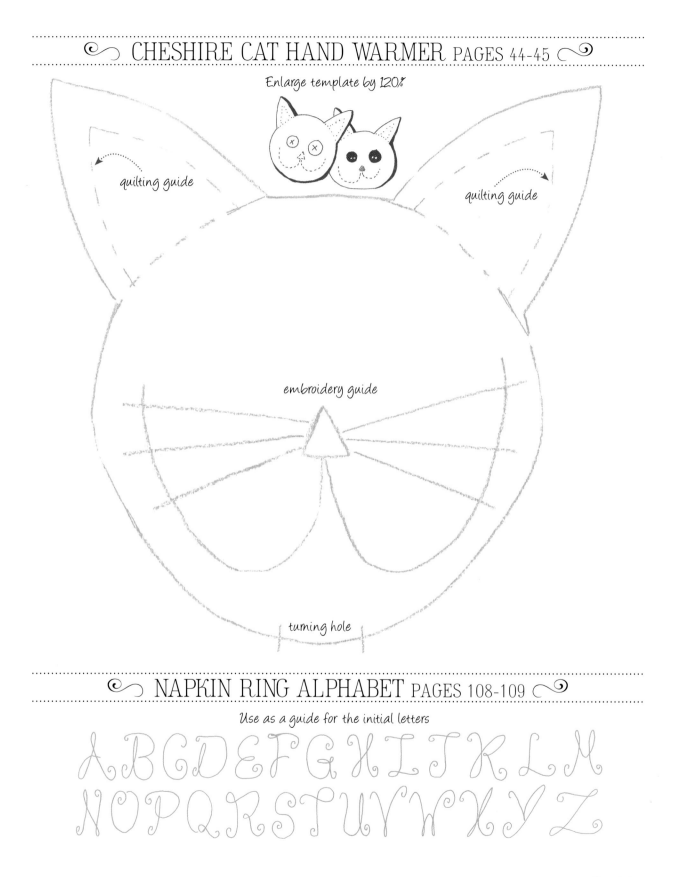

quilting guide

quilting guide

embroidery guide

turning hole

❧ NAPKIN RING ALPHABET PAGES 108-109 ❧

Use as a guide for the initial letters

ABCDEFGHIJKLM
NOPQRSTUVWXYZ

✎ HUMPTY DUMPTY DOORSTOP PAGES 40-43 ✎

Each square of the graph paper is equivalent to 2cm

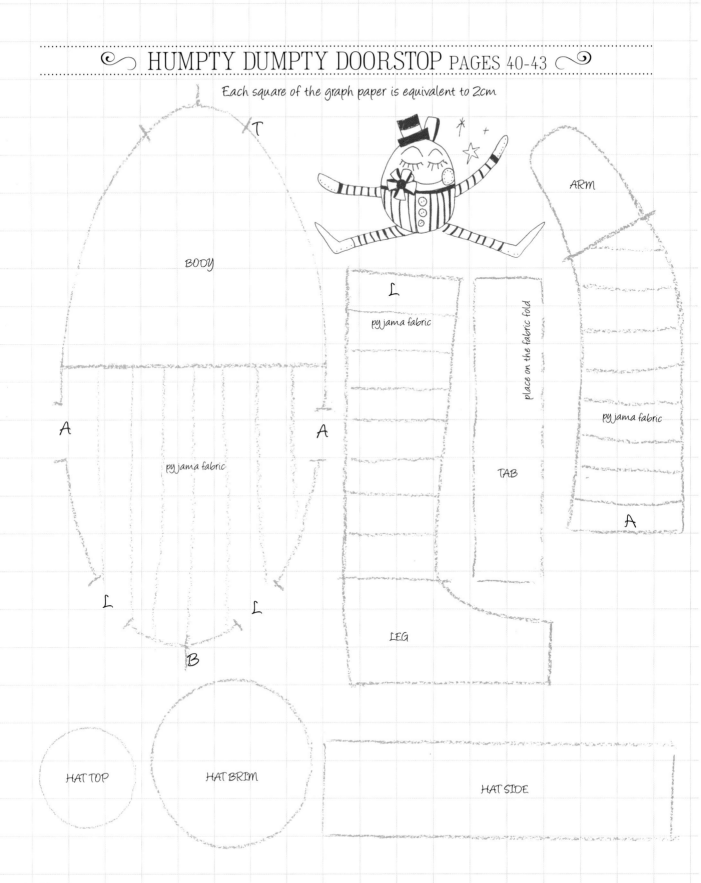

T

BODY

A

pyjama fabric

A

L

L

B

L

pyjama fabric

A

place on the fabric fold

TAB

ARM

pyjama fabric

A

LEG

HAT TOP

HAT BRIM

HAT SIDE

MARCH HARE'S HOUSE TEACOSY PAGES 104-5

Each square of the graph paper is equivalent to 2cm

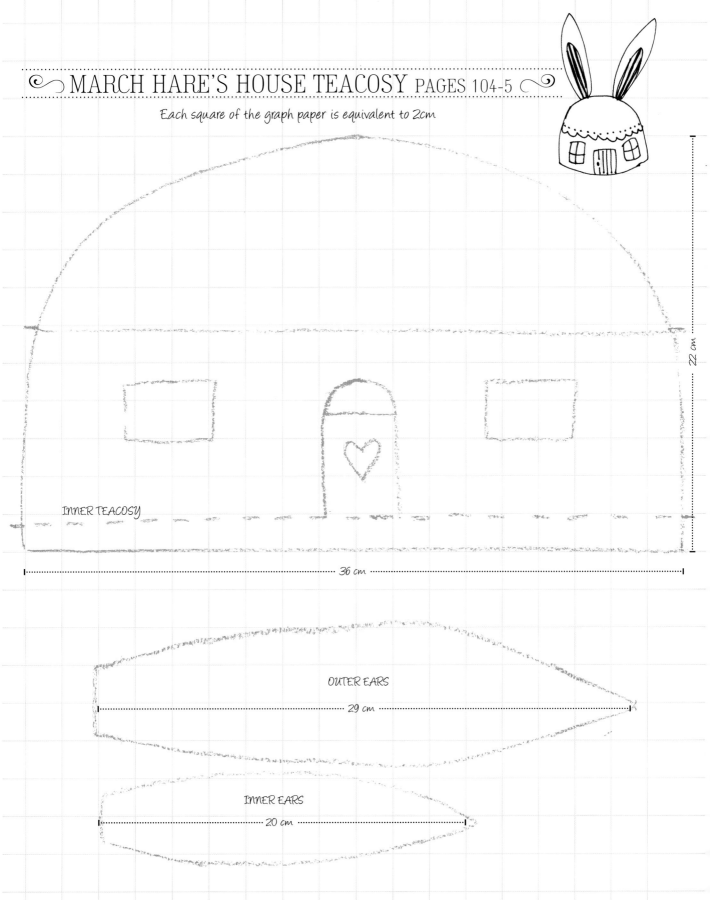

INNER TEACOSY

22 cm

36 cm

OUTER EARS

29 cm

INNER EARS

20 cm

Each square of the graph paper is equivalent to 2cm or enlarge by 200%

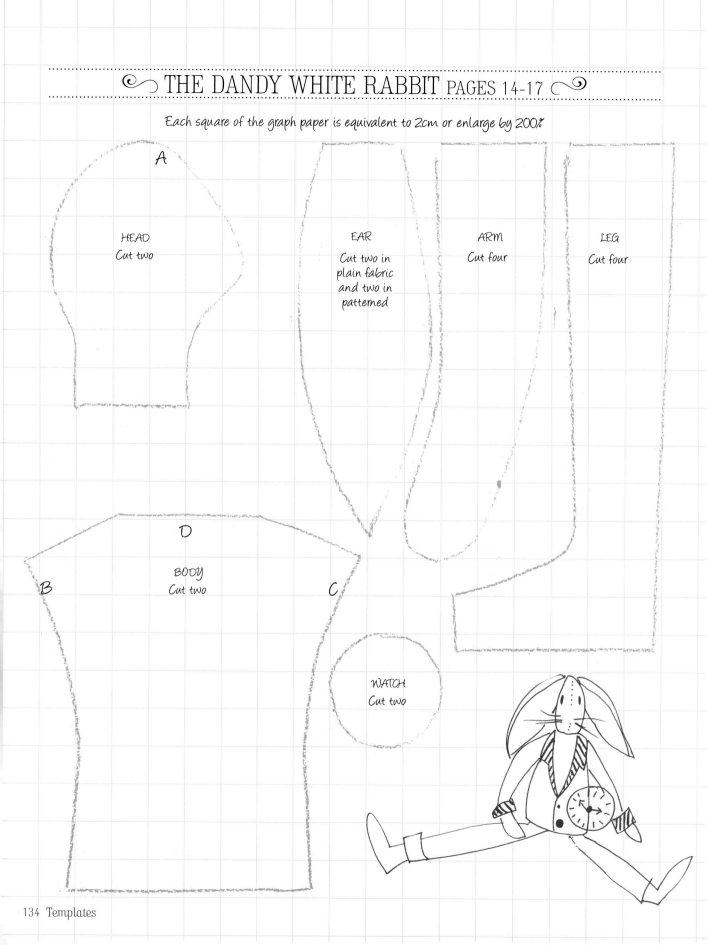

A

HEAD
Cut two

EAR

Cut two in
plain fabric
and two in
patterned

ARM
Cut four

LEG
Cut four

D

BODY
Cut two

B

C

WATCH
Cut two

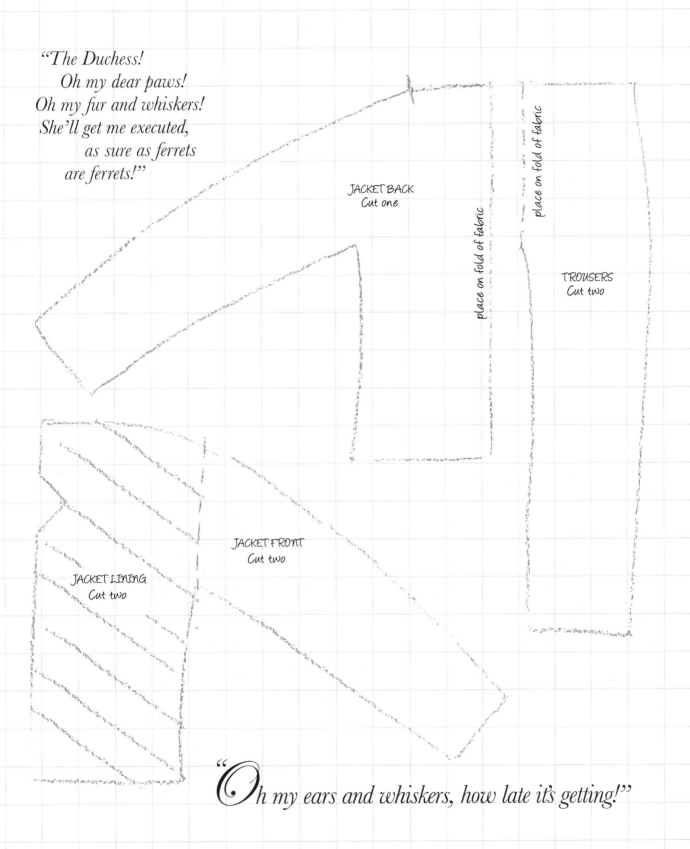

"*The Duchess!*
Oh my dear paws!
Oh my fur and whiskers!
She'll get me executed,
as sure as ferrets
are ferrets!"

JACKET BACK
Cut one

place on fold of fabric

place on fold of fabric

TROUSERS
Cut two

JACKET FRONT
Cut two

JACKET LINING
Cut two

"*Oh my ears and whiskers, how late it's getting!*"

✌ INVITATION CUSHION PAGES 26-28 ✌

Each square of the graph paper is equivalent to 4cm

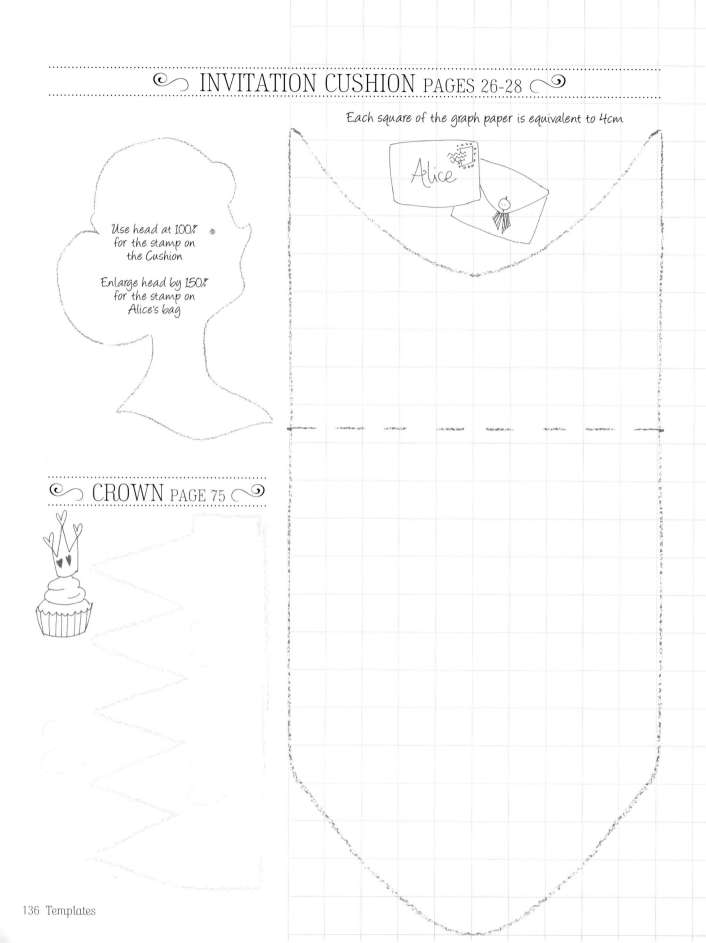

Use head at 100%
for the stamp on
the Cushion

Enlarge head by 150%
for the stamp on
Alice's bag

Alice

✌ CROWN PAGE 75 ✌

Each square of the graph paper is equivalent to 4cm

Each square of the graph paper is equivalent to 4cm

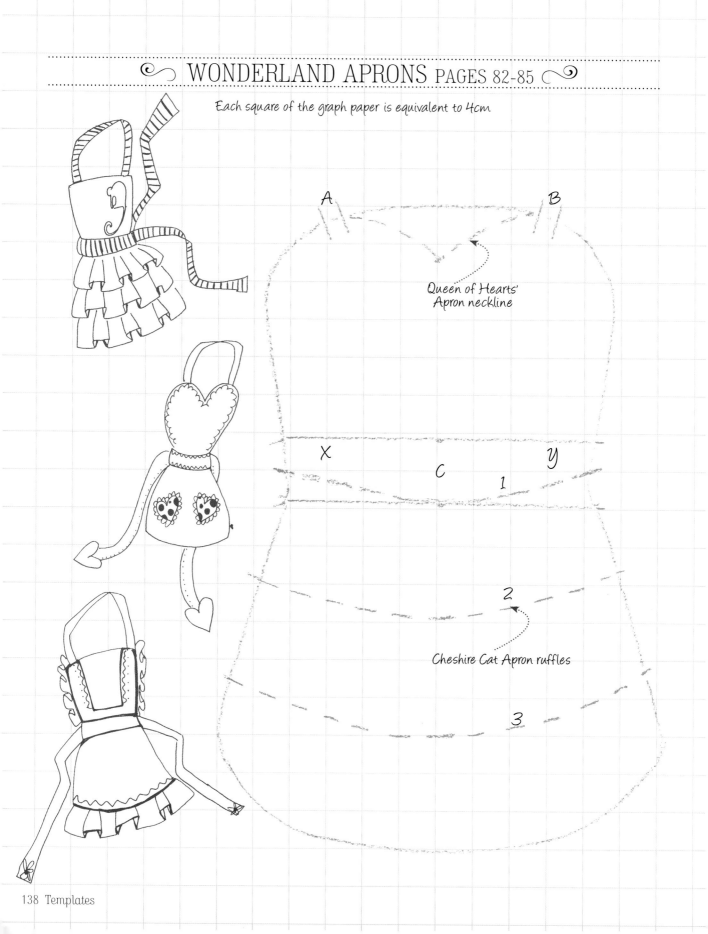

Each square of the graph paper is equivalent to 4cm

A   B

Queen of Hearts'
Apron neckline

X   𝒴

            C

                1

                    2

Cheshire Cat Apron ruffles

                    3

CHESHIRE CAT
APRON MOTIF
Enlarge cat by 150%

QUEEN OF HEARTS'
APRON POCKET
Enlarge by 170%

WAISTBAND TIES
Enlarge by 170%

Directory

*W*hilst making the projects in this book we found many inspiring places for supplies and ideas. Here are some of our favourites.

SUPPLIERS

Barnett Lawson
Behind a plain door and down some stairs is this amazing treasure trove of trimmings.
16–17 Little Portland Street
London W1W 8NE
020 7636 8591
www.bltrimmings.com

Blade Rubber
12 Bury Place
London WC1A 2JL
020 7831 4123
www.bladerubberstamps.co.uk

The Bead Shop Manchester
One of the best jewellery making resources you can find online.
18 Upper Chorlton Road
Manchester M16 7RN
0161 232 7356
www.the-beadshop.co.uk

The Cloth House
47 & 98 Berwick Street
London W1F 0QJ
020 7437 5155
020 7287 1555
www.clothhouse.com

Dolls House Parade
4a Royal Parade
Chislehurst
Kent BR7 6NR
020 8295 0688
www.dollshouseparade.net

The Dover Book Shop
18 Earlham Street
London WC2H 9LG
020 7836 2111
www.doverbooks.co.uk

eBay
It's a brilliant way to snap up bargains on vintage china. Remember to look for pretty brands such as Shelly, Tuscan China, Foley and Wedgwood.
www.ebay.com

Hobbycraft
The perfect place for general craft and cookery decoration supplies; See website for your local store.
01202 596100
www.hobbycraft.co.uk

Klein's
An Aladdin's cave of fantastic trims so give yourself some time to have a good old rummage.
5 Noel Street
London W1F 8GD
020 7437 6162
www.kleins.co.uk

Lakeland Plastics
One of the largest kitchenware retailers in the UK, they are great for specialist items such as unusual cake moulds and edible glitter. See website for your local store.
01539 488100
www.lakeland.co.uk

Liberty
If you're ever feeling stressed shopping on Oxford Street, five minutes in the beautiful environs of Liberty will calm you again.
Great Marlborough Street
London W1B 5AH
www.liberty.co.uk

London Graphic Centre
Supplier of a huge range of general art and graphic supplies.
16–18 Shelton Street
London WC2H 9JL
020 7759 4500
www.londongraphics.co.uk

MacCulloch & Wallis
Just off Oxford street this store is a great place to get fine fabrics, millinery goods and trims.
25–26 Dering Street
London W1S 1AT
020 7629 0311
www.macculloch-wallis.co.uk

Mrs Stokes Vintage China
Mrs Stokes scours car boot sales and auction houses so you don't have to. An amazing array of vintage teasets and other treats are on her website.
www.mrsstokes.com

Myriad Natural Toys
A great selection of 100% wool felt in a myriad of colours.
01725 517085
www.myriadonline.co.uk

Paperchase
The flagship store has a whole floor dedicated to handmade papers, cards and craft supplies.
12 Alfred Place
London WC1E 7EB
020 7467 6200
www.paperchase.co.uk

Shepton Mallet Flea Market

This huge indoor and outdoor market provides a plethora of antiques. Get there early!
www.sheptonflea.com

Squires Kitchen Sugarcraft

Online shop boasting a massive range of cake decorating goodies
0845 617 1810
www.squires-shop.com

The Trimming Company

Wonderful online resource for simanay and hat-making supplies.
www.thetrimmingcompany.com

V.V. Rouleaux

This shop is a great place to visit and gain inspiration for any sewing project, the store is cram-packed with the most beautiful ribbons and trims.
49 Hallam Street
London W1U 2QD
020 7224 5179
www.vvrouleaux.com

INSPIRATION

Bailey Tomlin Hats

Designer Bridget Tomlin truly is the Mad Hatter, her fantastical designs are the perfect accessory for any tea party.
www.baileytomlin.com

Beatrix Ong

Beatrix's London shoe shop has taken inspiration from Alice with her giant knitted clock, stack of playing cards and even a Cheshire Cat on the back wall.
8 Newburgh Street
(just off Carnaby Street)
London W1F 7RJ
020 3463 7369
www.beatrixong.com

Bridport Old Bookshop

Possibly the most wonderful bookshop in the world, this hidden gem is full of vintage books specialising in children's stories.
11 South Street
Bridport
Dorset DT6 3NR
01308 425689

Laduree

The best macaroons in the world! A taste of heaven in every morsel.
87–135 Brompton Road
London SW1X 7XL
0871 971 4193
www.laduree.fr

Les Trois Garçons

As soon as you walk through the door of this restaurant you feel like you have entered into another world, surrounded by theatrical stuffed animals dressed in crowns and jewels. The food also out of this world!
1 Club Row
London E1 6JX
020 7613 1924
www.loungelover.co.uk

Thelermont Hupton

The place for surreal homeware design injecting humour into every piece, such as the Stuck On You hooks. They are well worth a look.
www.thelermonthupton.com

Christ Church College, Oxford

This is where Lewis Carroll studied and lived, you can visit the university and its Great Hall.
St Aldates
Oxford OX1 1DP
01865 276150
www.chch.ox.ac.uk

Alice Tour

Bring Victorian England and the world of Lewis Carroll back to life with local historian and author of Alice In Waterland, Mark Davies.
www.oxfordwaterwalks.co.uk

The Alice Shop

This actual shop was featured in Through the Looking Glass and is full of Alice treasures.
83 St Aldates
Oxford OX1 1RA
01865 723793
www.aliceinwonderlandshop.co.uk

Alice Sculptures

These unique brass sculptures were commissioned by George Delacorte in honour of his wife, Margarita. A wonderful place to visit if you are ever in NYC.
East Side, Central Park,
New York
www.centralpark.com

The Lewis Carroll Society

Founded in 1969 to bring together people with an interest in Charles Dodgson, to promote his life and works.
www.lewiscarrollsociety.org.uk

Hannah Read-Baldrey

To see what Hannah's been up to when not book-bound, log on to
www.couturecraft.blogspot.com

Sylvie Fleury

www.sylviefleury.com

Tim Walker

An inspiring photographer who loves creating images inspired by fairytales on a grand scale.
www.timwalkerphotography.com

Tiffany Mumford

An equally inspiring photographer, who we worked with to create this book.
www.tiffanymumford.com

"*A large rose-tree stood near the entrance of the garden: the roses growing on it were white, but there were three gardeners at it, busily painting them red. Alice thought this a very curious thing*"

Index

~ Hannah & Christine ~

With thanks

To Jane, Lisa & Helen at Quadrille for their guidance, encouragement and belief in us and our mad ideas. To Tiffany for her amazing photography and for reining us in when our ideas went that little too crazy.

Hannah I have to thank my amazing parents, Matthew & Stephanie, for allowing us to take over their house for two weeks. My wonderful husband, Brendan, for (constantly) living in our mad house with my crazy things coming and going. And to our family cat, Harold, who will be very much missed.

Christine Thank you so much to my remarkable parents for all their support and belief in me and my endeavours. To mum for her roadtesting and research, to dad for his wooden flamingos and problem-solving and to both of them for giving me my skills and knowledge of all things craft. To my wonderful sister Jo, Ian, Oliver and Elliot for their support and slipper-trying-on. To Jake, Kirsty, Laura, Stuart, Matt, Hannah, Cath and Lottie, I promise I'll talk about something else from now on!